JURASSIC COAST JUSTICE

CW00821807

TRUE STORIES OF MURDER, MYSTERY AND MUTINY FROM DORSET AND DEVON'S DARK PAST

Mark Bridgeman

Watermill Books

Published in 2023 by
Watermill Books
Mill Street
Aberfeldy
Perthshire PH15 2BG
www.aberfeldywatermill.com

British Library Cataloguing-in-Publication Data

A catalogue record for this book is available from the British Library

ISBN 978-0-9957795-6-3

Designed by EMB Graphics, Aberfeldy

Printed and bound in the UK by Bell & Bain Ltd, Glasgow

JURASSIC COAST
JUSTICE

TRUE STORIES OF MURDER, MYSTERY AND MUTINY FROM DORSET AND DEVON'S DARK PAST

Mark Bridgeman

Watermill Books

CONTENTS

INTRODUCTION

Justice will not be served until those
who are unaffected are as outraged as those who are.
Benjamin Franklin

Surely, the light under which we examine the evolution of the
English legal system, and the resulting fight for justice, burns
brighter in the counties of Devon and Dorset than anywhere
else on these islands.

Whether it be criminal, social, or political justice, the rolling
hills, picturesque villages and market towns that inhabit the
area that has come to be known as the Jurassic Coast bear
witness to a catalogue of crimes and injustices that offer a
fascinating insight into the day-to-day struggles of life in rural
England of years gone by.

This book opens the door to a world of poverty, poor working
conditions, social injustice, and attitudes which caused some to
turn to crime, when life seemed to offer little alternative, except
perhaps an increasing dependence on alcohol. Yet, in among
the darker stories, there are inspiring tales of men and women
who refused to accept their lot in life, instead, standing up for

their rights at a time when many of us might have chosen an easier path. Rights which we enjoy today and for which their sacrifice must not be forgotten.

Crime, and therefore justice (or the lack of it), can take many forms. Jurassic Coast Justice examines crimes of anger, greed, desperation, temptation, and circumstance. Some of the crimes featured here might not even be considered an offence today. Occasionally, the justice meted out in these stories may seem too harsh by today's standards, or in some cases too lenient. Every reader will have a different opinion.

The timeless and picturesque beauty of the Devon and Dorset landscape may have served to camouflage centuries of crime and injustice, but it also inspired people to stand tall like the Jurassic coastline and speak out against the injustice they observed.

As long ago as 1645, tiring of both Royalist and Parliamentary troops plundering their livestock and crops, the farmers and villagers of Dorset united under the banner of the 'Clubman' and clashed with Cromwell's forces at the Battle of Hambledon Hill. Armed with clubs, scythes, shovels, and anything else they could lay their hands on, the clubman fought underneath a flag carrying the motif:

> *If you offer to plunder or take our cattle,*
> *Be assured we will bid you battle.*

Mark Bridgeman
www.markbridgemanauthor.co.uk

MURDER WILL OUT!
THE WEYMOUTH MYSTERY

When women are secret, they are secret indeed
Thomas Hardy

Justice weighed heavily on the minds of Britons in 1792. More than three hundred separate petitions against the slave trade were presented to William Pitt the Younger in Parliament, the first colony for freed slaves was created, and the London Corresponding Society was formed to advocate the need for universal suffrage, secret ballots, and annual parliaments. However, these potent aspirations, intended to help accomplish democracy and justice for the masses, would take many years to reach fruition.

Similarly, justice in a heinous murder committed during that very same year would also take many decades to be achieved. Even then, it was a very peculiar kind of justice.

If there was a perfect night to get away with murder, Thursday 26th April 1792 might have seemed to be it. Dark and cold on the streets of Weymouth, the heavy and continual rain had deterred many from venturing outdoors and the faint moonlight was obscured by cloud cover. The High Street, Boot Lane, the quay, and the old wooden Harbour Bridge were quiet and cloaked in misty shadow. A heinous murder was about to be committed; the perpetrators would then utilise the dark night and late hour to coldheartedly hide their foul deed.

A young jeweller and engraver, Thomas Lloyd Morgan, had spent that Thursday evening in Weymouth drinking with a friend. Around the hour of eleven, the twenty-two-year-old Morgan, together with his associate Hardy, a farmer from the village of Chickerell, both decided to visit the only brothel in Weymouth. They left the public house) and walked with their horses to the nearby 'house of ill fame', as they were then referred to. Hardy tied up his horse outside and the two men entered the den of iniquity. Once inside, they were greeted by Priscilla Guppy, the proprietor. In her early twenties, Priscilla, who appeared to display poor personal hygiene (a factor that was later to standi in her favour!), offered the two men a drink. Along with one, or possibly two, other men believed to there at the time, the group seem to have entered into a fierce argument, perhaps over money; or maybe as a result of drink-inflamed tempers.

As a result of the struggle, a savage blow from a blunt and heavy object crashed down on Thomas Morgan's head, smashing his skull, inflicting severe trauma, which rapidly resulted in his death. However, the incumbents of the house did not panic in the face of their awful deed. Instead, a cunning and calculated plan was quickly hatched, and a lifelong pact was agree to.

Thomas Morgan's watch and gold chain were removed along, no doubt, with any money he may have kept about his person. His blood-soaked body was then tightly wrapped in a large linen sheet. It appears that Priscilla Guppy had been ironing the establishment's bed linen and a supply was kept nearby. The body, now safely obscured, was carried outside and carefully placed across the saddle of the farmer, Hardy's, horse, which was still tethered outside in the street. It was now sometime between the hour of 11pm on Thursday 26th April and 4am the following morning.

The sinister party led Hardy's horse, with Thomas Morgan's body still slumped across it, away from Boot Lane and down towards the harbour. The group had hoped, by transporting the body a suitable distance from the house of ill fame, that any subsequent investigation would fail to link Morgan's death with the illicit premises. The group intended to carry the body, across the wooden harbour bridge, to Melcombe Regis and there dispose of it into the waters of the harbour. It was hoped that the body might sink, or perhaps even be washed away to some other place where a connection with Weymouth could not be readily made.

The footways were quiet, and the night was dark. The murderous group managed to reach the wooden harbour bridge and cross without difficulty. However, on reaching the Melcombe side of the bridge, they overheard the unmistakeable sound of voices somewhere close by. In the dark of night, and with an enveloping mist from the nearby harbour, the group had no idea from how far away the voices came, or from which direction. In a moment of panic, they pushed the body from the horse, and, with a muffled thud, it rolled to the side of the road and came to rest. Quickly, the group returned to the original scene of the crime in the High Street without being observed. Although their plan had not been a complete success, they appeared to have escaped unseen. Congratulating themselves, they made a lifelong pact, agreeing never to divulge their awful secret to another living soul.

Between four and five o'clock the following morning, a labourer on his way to work noticed a strange object in the half-light, lying on the side of the road close to the wooden bridge. He cautiously approached the motionless bloodied parcel and carefully loosened it. To his horror, he immediately realised it was the disfigured body of a man. He reported his gruesome find to the local police constable. With no official Dorset police force existing until the 1850s, back in the 1790s each town was required to employ its own constable, magistrate, and coroner. An alarm was raised, rumours quickly spread, and a state of panic soon gripped the town. An unknown killer lurked among them.

As daylight dawned on the Friday morning, a search for clues was ordered. Fortunately for the investigating officials, this would yield results almost immediately. The killers, it seems, had left a careless clue in their wake.

Either completely unseen in the dark, or perhaps wrongly assuming that the rain of the previous week would cover their tracks, the murderers of Thomas Morgan had failed to notice that a steady trail of blood had dripped from the body of the dead man during its journey on horseback from the door of the brothel to the very spot it was discovered on the north side of the harbour bridge. The police constable, together with several volunteers, carefully retraced the trail of blood spots directly to the door of the house in which the murder had been committed.

Known to the police as a house of ill repute, suspicion immediately fell on the occupants and upon those who had visited during the previous evening. An immediate coroner's inquest was ordered, which commenced with the chosen jury members viewing the murdered man's body (as was a requirement at the time). Eighteenth-century inquests usually took place in the nearest public house, as these buildings tended to offer practical advantages, such as accommodation for visiting magistrates and witnesses, a sufficiently sized public room, and a kitchen or dining table large enough upon which to display the body. The inquest in this case most probably had occurred at the nearby Boot Inn, and almost certainly within two days of the body being found. The need for a rapid inquest, in the days before the ability to refrigerate a decaying corpse existed, would have been all too obvious for those in attendance – particularly during the warmer months.

The events were recorded in the *Hampshire Chronicle* on 7th May 1792:

Last Thursday a young man, of the name Thomas Lloyd Morgan, an engraver, in company with one Hardy, a farmer, in the neighbourhood, after having spent the evening together, went to a house of ill-fame about eleven at night, and the next morning, about four, the unfortunate Morgan was found murdered on the bridge, with his skull terribly fractured, and many other marks of violence on his body. The coroner's inquest brought in their verdict of wilful murder by some person or persons unknown. Two women and a man named Robert Thedham, belonging to the house above-mentioned, were immediately taken into custody, as likewise the farmer with whom he was in company; they were all committed to the county prison to take their trials at the ensuing assizes. Morgan was a native of Leominster, Herefordshire, where he has parents now living in respectable circumstances.

With no legal requirement for autopsies or death certificates, the body of Thomas Morgan was buried immediately. In cases of murder, this haste often helped a guilty murderer escape justice, as the evidence of their crime was quite literally 'dead and buried'.

Meanwhile, Priscilla Guppy, Hardy, a man named Robert Thedham, another customer by the name of Tiddins, and one other woman, were arrested and placed in Dorchester Gaol to await trial.

While the trail of blood, leading from the house of ill repute to the dumping place of the body, seemed to strongly suggest the scene of the murder, there was no direct evidence to link any of the arrested group with the killing. Priscilla Guppy claimed to know nothing of the incident and Hardy's maid servant even testified to the fact that he had been home in bed asleep at the supposed time of the murder. And so, there was to be no justice for the family of Thomas Morgan.

Although Morgan's family were referred to as 'living in respectable circumstances' in the above article, they do not appear to have been able to afford a decent burial for their son. Morgan was buried in the churchyard of the Parish Church of St Mary's in St Mary's Street, Melcombe Regis in what was recorded at the time as a pauper's grave.

With all Morgan's worldly possessions probably removed from his murdered body by his killers, there does not seem to have been enough money available to pay for a headstone. Fortunately, however, a public collection managed to raise sufficient funds and shortly afterwards a stone was placed at his graveside, inscribed as follows:

This stone was erected by Public Subscription in remembrance of the cruel murder committed on the body of Lloyd Morgan, who lies here, on the 27th April, aged 22.

Here mingling with my fellow clay,
I wait the awful judgement day,
And there my murderer shall appear,
Although escaped from justice here.

And there the investigation stalled. Lacking sufficient evidence, the arrested individuals were released without charge. Although rumours and suspicions continued for many years, no proof ever came to light to warrant further investigations or arrests.

Until one day, that is, many, many years later.

In mid-November 1857, sixty-five years after Thomas Morgan's murder, an inmate at the Union Workhouse in Wyke Road, Weymouth, called for a witness to hear her confession. The inmate, an elderly lady in her nineties, was destitute, and had been in the workhouse for many years. Now on her deathbed, she summoned the strength to finally make her peace with the Lord.

The story of her deathbed confession was recorded in several newspapers, including the *Bridport News*, which documented her story, and went to great lengths to locate anyone in the town who might recall the incident sixty-five years earlier:

WEYMOUTH. MURDER WILL OUT!

A great deal of excitement has been created during the past week, in consequence of rumour that an old woman named Priscilla Guppy on her deathbed has confessed that she was a participator in a most foul and cruel murder, committed more than half century ago, but the real perpetrators of which at that time could not be discovered.

The particulars of this dark deed we have gathered from the testimony of many old persons still living, and who can distinctly recollect the circumstance, that about the period mentioned great alarm was felt in the town in consequence of the discovery of a human body wrapt in a linen sheet, lying near the foot of the old bridge, on the Melcombe Regis side of the harbour…

…suspicion was at once raised to the guilty parties; the deceased woman, Hardy, Tiddins, and others who visited the house of ill-fame were at once arrested and brought before the Tribunal at Dorchester, but the evidence failed clearly to substantiate the charge and they were acquitted.

Although no legal justice was forthcoming in this case, it seems a different sort of retribution was handed down to those behind

Thomas Morgan's death. Priscilla Guppy lived her remaining
years in destitution and misery, fearing what awaited her after
death. Hardy became a changed man and, he too, lived out the
remainder of his life in misery. Even the horse used to carry
the body of the murdered man seems to have paid a heavy
price. The *Bridport News* continued its moral warning to all those
hoping to evade the long arm of the law:

*The hand of conscience works wonders. Hardy is said never to have been
a happy man afterwards; of the other parties one family is now entirely
extinct. An anecdote is even told of the horse which we believe is true, that
so sensitive was the animal of the deed which had been committed, that it
would never pass that house afterwards, and his master was compelled to get
rid of him.*

*A few days ago, (20th November 1857), the last of the survivors of those
supposed to be participators in the dreadful deed, died, Priscila Guppy. On
her death bed, her state of mind was truly frightful; she had attained a
great age being upwards of 90. It is stated that previous to her decease she
confessed she was a participator in the murder, having beat Thomas Morgan
in the head with a flat piece of iron or heater, such as is used in ironing linen.
She implored the Divine Creator to have mercy on her soul and forgive the
sins she had committed. We understand that she stated that when she was
arraigned before the bar of justice at the trial, she had the gold watch and
chain of the murdered man concealed in the hair of her head.*

It appears that the magistrates had no intention of searching her
unwashed and lice-ridden hair for evidence. Had they done so,
they would have discovered the murdered man's gold chain and
watch.

In her deathbed confession, Priscilla Guppy also revealed how
Hardy had been able to provide an alibi for the time of the
murder:

*After the commission of the crime, Hardy went home to his own house and
immediately upon entering, put the clock back two hours. He then retired*

to rest, and a short time afterwards awoke his servant and told her to go downstairs and see what was the time. Then she returned and told her master quite innocently the hour, not knowing that the clock had been altered. She was brought forward at the trial, and thus her testimony to his being home at the time the crime was supposed to have been committed thus led to Hardy's acquittal. The murdered man was interred with great respect in the churchyard of St. Mary's Church, where, to this day, may be seen his tombstone.

Although Thomas Lloyd Morgan did not receive justice in his lifetime, the mystery of his murder was at last solved. However, he was not left to rest in peace.

During some alterations to St Mary's Church, a number of gravestones were removed and reset elsewhere. Morgan's memorable headstone, lamenting the lack of justice he was to receive in his lifetime, now resides in the paving at the east end of the nave:

> *Here mingling with my fellow clay,*
> *I wait the awful judgement day,*
> *And there my murderer shall appear,*
> *Although escaped from justice here.*

It seems, after all, the ominous verse was correct and did foreshadow the time at which the killers of Thomas Morgan would meet their judgement day.

THE WHIT MONDAY MURDER
(PART ONE)

*Indifference to fate which, though it often makes a villain of a man,
is the basis of his sublimity when it does not.*

Thomas Hardy, *Far From the Madding Crowd* (1874)

If you had joined the throngs of Victorian tourists enjoying
the early summer sunshine visiting picturesque Corfe Castle on
Whit Monday in May 1882, you too might have witnessed two
colourful travelling musicians entertaining the crowds.

Dennis Riley and Henry Wright had travelled from Wareham
in the hope of earning a few shillings entertaining the
holidaymakers with a series of songs describing infamous
murders of the day. These ditties, known as 'murder ballads'
were a popular form of musical entertainment during the late
Victorian era, although considered in poor taste by the politer
elements of society. Riley and Wright wandered the busy streets
and alleyways of Corfe Castle all day, singing their rough ballads
about the Phoenix Park murders (the fatal stabbings, just three
weeks earlier, of Lord Cavendish and Thomas Burke in Dublin
by members of the Irish National Invincibles), and the execution
of Dr Lamson, who had been hanged at the beginning of the
year for the poisoning of his brother-in-law.

After earning enough money for food and drink, the two men
indulged themselves at the Castle Inn, in East Street.

Around 4 o'clock, they were refused any more drink by the landlord, and decided instead to walk in the direction of Swanage, in the hope of doing much the same on the following day.

However, the two men, their tempers no doubt inflamed with alcohol and the heat of the day, appear to have entered into a violent argument. Henry Wright was heard to say that he would 'do for that bastard, by and bye', before being witnessed punching Dennis Riley. Another witness, James Smith, a local bricklayer, observed the commotion from the window of his mother's cottage on East Street. He rushed outside to assist. With Dennis Riley already lying on the grass beside the road, Henry Wright was seen holding a large stone above his head, which he then used to rain a mighty blow down onto Riley's skull. Before he could do so again, two passers-by, together with James Smith, wrestled with Wright, taking the stone from his clutches and pushing him against the nearby stone wall. While a woman from one of the cottages attempted to attend to Riley's savage injuries, two of the witnesses manhandled Henry Wright to the home of local police Sergeant Absolom Wiles, who placed him in custody.

Henry Wright was locked in the cells at Wareham police station while Sergeant Wiles hurried to the scene of the crime. However, by the time he reached the location, Riley had been carried to the nearby Castle Inn where he passed away shortly afterwards as a result of his severe injuries. Sergeant Wiles removed Dennis Riley's personal possessions from his clothing, then gave instructions that the corpse be kept at the Castle Inn for further examination. He then returned to the police station and questioned Henry Wright:

What is your name?

Henry Wright

Henry Wright, I am charging you with the murder of Dennis Riley, the deceased. I am cautioning you to be careful in your reply, as whatever you say will be used against you.

If he is dead, he is dead, Wright replied, *He'll die but once. I did give him a crack on the head with a stone.*

Although the suspect's guilt might have appeared obvious to Sergeant Wiles and to the witnesses, a coroner's inquest and trial would still be needed. Would Henry Wright receive a fair defence in court, if his confession to Sergeant Wiles had been obtained without a full explanation of his rights having been first explained to him, and without a witness present?

The vexed question regarding the relative merits of statements or confessions given to police officers by suspects, and then subsequently repeated in court, had recently been addressed by the Metropolitan Police. It must be remembered that, in 1882, the police constabulary in Dorset was still a relatively new one, having only been established in 1856. Today, we might expect to receive some standardisation in the formal charge read to us by a police officer, but this was certainly not the case in 1882. Sergeant Wiles was perfectly entitled to charge his prisoner using whatever language he chose fit, and without the presence of a witness to corroborate any answers given. Although the Metropolitan Police had recently issued *The Police Code*, a booklet intended to guide officers' actions, the document was intended as a statement of best practice only and held no statutory authority. By 1882, the booklet had filtered down to the Dorset Police Constabulary and Sergeant Wiles was almost certainly one of the first officers to adopt some, if not all, of its recommendations for cautioning prisoners.

In the introduction to *The Police Code*, written by the High Court judge Sir Henry Hawkins, police officers were advised as follows:

On arresting a man, a Constable ought simply to read his warrant, or tell the accused the nature of the charge upon which he is arrested, leaving it to the person so arrested to say anything or nothing as he pleases. For a Constable to press any accused person to say anything with reference to the crime of which he is accused is very wrong.

There is, however, no objection to a Constable listening to any mere voluntary statement which a prisoner desires to make, and repeating such statement in evidence; nor is there any objection to his repeating in evidence any conversation he may have heard between the prisoner and any other person. But he ought not by anything he says or does, to invite or encourage an accused person to make any statement, without first cautioning him that he is not bound to say anything tending to criminate himself, and that anything he says may be used against him.

Perhaps the best maxim for a Constable to bear in mind with respect to an accused person is, 'Keep your eyes and your ears open, and your mouth shut'.

It would be another thirty years before a formally and uniformly worded caution would be adopted nationwide. In the meantime, Henry Wright would need to rely on the word of Sergeant Wiles to ensure he was justly tried. Firstly, however, came the formality of the inquest.

An inquest was hastily arranged at the Castle Inn. A jury was assembled and was presented with the evidence collected from several witnesses as well as from the body of Dennis Riley. After a short hearing Wright was found 'Guilty of wilful murder' by the inquest jury. The decision of an inquest was not a legal conviction of guilt, however. That would require a murder trial.

Amid intense public interest a trial date was set for Thursday 20th July 1882 at the Dorchester Assizes.

On the day of the trial, with the public gallery full, an excited crowd gathered outside, all confidently expecting Henry Wright's guilt to be confirmed. Mr Justice Henry Lopes, a native of Maristow in Devon, opened the proceedings with the grandly named Mr Wiliam Molesworth St. Aubyn MP, and Mr F Vincent Budge prosecuting for the Crown. Henry Wright was defended by a flamboyant and interesting young barrister by the name of Charles Matthews, whose advocacy would prove crucial during the proceedings. Mr Justice Lopes had personally arranged for Charles Matthews to defend Henry Wright on a pro bono basis, under the assumption that the defendant may enter a plea of insanity.

Charles Matthews had been born in New York, the son of a Broadway actress. After studying at Eton College, he joined chambers in London. Only thirty-two at the time of this trial, he would later go on to become a leading Crown prosecutor, acting in many of the era's most famous trials including the prosecution of the Jameson Raiders, Oscar Wilde v The Marquess of Queensberry, and the case of Kitty Byron (one of Edwardian Britain's most notorious murders). An acquaintance of King Edward VII, and then King George V, he would also become Britain's first Director of Public Prosecutions in 1908. Cases involving Charles Matthews always promised much entertainment for the public gallery, and were described by the journalist Bernald Falk as:

Tense and emotional as that of a playhouse in which some moving drama is being played.

Meanwhile, the weight of evidence seemed to be stacked against Henry Wright. With his apparent confession to Sergeant Wiles, it seemed that even the energy of Charles Matthews could not prevent his client from going to the gallows.

The charge was read as the courtroom fell into an expectant silence:

Henry Wright, also known as Joseph James Kingsford, you are charged that you did feloniously, wilfully, and with malice aforethought, kill and murder a certain male person, whose supposed name was Dennis Riley, at Corfe Castle on this 29th May, 1882. How do you plead?

Not guilty, your honour.

During the preparation for the trial, Wright had revealed that his real name was, in fact, Joseph James Kingsford, that he had previously been employed as a baker's assistant, and that he was thirty-three years of age.

His plea of not guilty, despite the weight of evidence, was not unsurprising. Defendants in Victorian trials were usually advised to plead not guilty; thus, offering the presiding judge a wider range of possible punishments should they be subsequently found guilty. An admission of guilt would offer little room for manoeuvre, other than a sentence of death.

With the preliminaries completed, the prosecution called their first witness, Jane Miller, who kept a lodging house in North Street, Wareham. She testified that Henry Wright and Dennis Riley:

Had come to my house and taken a room on three o'clock on the afternoon of Sunday 28th May. They stayed with me until the Monday morning at about nine o'clock, when they left. They were travelling singers and told me they were going to Corfe Castle.

Thank you, Mrs Miller.

Charles Matthews cross-examined for the defence, *And did they appear to be friendly towards each other, Mrs Miller?*

Yes, sir. I never heard them have any dispute.

The prosecution interrupted the cross-examination at this point, *But, surely, Mrs Miller, they were only with you for a short period of time? Surely, even the worst of enemies would not be expected to fall out within a matter of a few hours?*

No, sir. I suppose not. answered the witness.

Thank you, you may return to your seat, Mrs Miller.

Next came the crucial evidence of Robert Seymour. He had passed the two men in East Street on the day of the murder, walking in the direction of Swanage. On behalf of the Crown, Mr St. Aubyn began:

Mr Seymour, what is your occupation?

I am a labourer, sir.

And what were you doing on the afternoon of the murder?

Well, sir, I passed the two men – the prisoner and the deceased – they was walking down the Swanage Road. The prisoner (he pointed to Henry Wright, who was sitting nonchalantly in the dock, looking down at the floor) told the other man to keep quiet, then he hit him with his fist. I begged him to desist from hitting the other man in case a policeman came by. He told me that he would 'do for that bastard by and bye.'

Thank you, Mr Seymour. And when did you next see the men?

I saw the body of the deceased in the Castle Inn, and I identified the prisoner at Wareham police station. It was the same man I had seen in the street.

Thank you, Mr Seymour.

Next to be called for the prosecution was John Snook, a carpenter with a workshop close to the scene of the murder:

Mr Snook, can you describe for the benefit of the court exactly what you saw on the 29th May last.

I was at work in my shop. About four o'clock I heard a noise outside. I looked outside and saw the prisoner sitting on the grass, about sixty feet away. About a quarter of an hour afterwards the deceased man came up, and I heard some words between the two men. Then they proceeded along the road in the direction of Swanage. After some distance the deceased man went from the middle of the road on to some grass and lay down near a stone wall.

And could you see him clearly, Mr Snook?

Yes, sir. He was lying with his forehead leaning on his hands, with his face towards the ground. His hat was off. The prisoner was some distance in front. He took a stone off the wall, turned round, and ran to where the deceased was lying. He took the stone in both hands and struck the deceased on the back of the head with it.

And what happened next, Mr Snook?

He picked up the stone again and struck the deceased again several times on the head, holding the stone in both hands as before. I ran up to the two men, and by that time another man called Smith was there. We caught hold of the prisoner and took him to the police station. We told the prisoner he had killed the other man, and he replied 'It served the bastard right! All such bastards should be served the same.'

Charles Matthews again cross-examined for the defence, *And did the defendant appear to be under the influence of drink, Mr Snook?*

No, sir, he did not appear the worse for drink.

Thank you, no further questions, my Lord.

The next witness, James Smith, the man who had assisted John Snook in tackling Henry Wright, explained his view of the events on that Whit Monday afternoon:

I saw a man lying with his face in his hands, from my mother's window. I went outside and saw that his head was exposed. Meanwhile, the prisoner returned with a very large stone, and struck the deceased on the head with much force.

The final two witnesses for the prosecution were able to confirm the death of Dennis Riley. Mary Ann Morris had attempted to help Riley as he lay bleeding on the ground:

He was struggling for life. I turned him on his back and he was then carried into the Castle Inn. I was with him until he died.

John Miller, the landlord of the Castle Inn, remembered the traumatic day well:

Both men came into my inn that day and drank. They left, then about three-quarters of an hour later the deceased man was brought to my house. He died within about five minutes.

Next came the crucial evidence of Sergeant Wiles, obtained during his conversation with Henry Wright at the police station. With no witness present, and no formal caution given, this testimony might be considered 'hearsay' today. Nevertheless, it carried much weight in 1882, as did the piece of evidence produced by the prosecution at this juncture in the proceedings:

I cautioned the prisoner to be careful in his reply, began Sergeant Wiles, *but he told me, 'If he is dead, he's dead. He'll die but once. I did give him a crack on the head with a stone. I am only sorry it was not a bigger one.'*

He then became agitated and proceeded to say, 'What I said is true, I only knew him a fortnight; and I will do so again to any man who tries to better me.'

Mr Molesworth St. Aubyn then produced several items of evidence for the court, the final one, no doubt saved for dramatic effect, created an audible gasp from the public gallery. Firstly, the mundane contents of Henry Wright's pockets were laid out on the evidence table - some sheet music, notepaper, and one penny piece, which seemed to be the sum total of the prisoner's worldly goods. Next, a large, bloodstained stone was lifted theatrically on to the table and thumped down with a resounding crash.

Gentleman of the jury, Mr St Aubyn announced, *this stone was recovered from the scene of the murder by the witness James Smith. It is covered in blood now, as it was then. The stone has been weighed to be thirteen-and-one-half pounds* (the combined weight of five cricket bats)*; it fitted into a hole in the wall from which it had been taken.*

With the obviously deadly nature of the large, bloodied stone, which had been strategically placed within easy view of the Grand Jury, the Crown's final piece of evidence seemed to have achieved its desired effect.

With the Crown's case now completed, it only remained for the uncontested expected medical evidence to be presented to the Grand Jury by Dr Woodruffe Daniel, the well-known Wareham surgeon.

THE WHIT MONDAY MURDER
(PART TWO)

Imputed madness, prisoned solitude,
And the Mind's canker in its savage mood

Lord Byron, *The Lament of Tasso*, 1817

Following the compelling prosecution evidence against
Henry Wright, came the results of the post-mortem. Dr
Woodruffe Daniel from Wareham was asked to explain his
findings to the all-male jury - it would be almost forty years
until female jurors were permitted at the Dorset Assizes.
In 1882, 'the fairer sex' were considered too emotional, of
generally lower intelligence than men, and likely to faint at
the graphic nature of the testimony given in certain trials.
At the first admission of women onto a jury in 1920, the
Western Daily Press rather condescendingly reported:

Ladies of the Jury! An innovation which has developed beyond what
some promoters of the feminist movement bargained for, and too far for
the good of the community.

However, in 1882, the delicate sensibilities of those ladies
in the public gallery were taken into account by the Mr
Justice Henry Lopes, who ordered, *All females to be cleared*
from the court!, so that Dr Woodruffe Daniel could begin his

testimony. There was some dissension from the gallery but the stern Justice Lopes, a former Conservative Member of Parliament, was in no mood for disagreement and banged his gavel impatiently until the courthouse was emptied of all female witnesses and members of the public. Finally, Dr Daniel was allowed to speak:

I made my post-mortem examination of the deceased on Whit Tuesday, with the assistance of Dr Webster. The only marks of violence were upon the head. There was a bruise on his right eye. On the back of the head there were two further wounds. They had penetrated quite through the scalp. I removed the scalp and found a fracture of the skull, six-and-a-half inches in length, extending in a zigzag direction, from two inches above the left eye to about one inch below the right ear. The injuries were sufficient to cause death.

And what force would be required to create such injuries, Doctor? enquired Justice Lopes.

Considerable violence must have been used to cause these wounds, in my opinion.

It was now time for the second act of the drama to begin – the case for the defence.

Charles Matthews's presentation of the defence's case would need to be passionate and articulate, if he was to persuade the jury that the verdict against Henry Wright should not be one of murder, but one of insanity. He began by immediately recalling Dr Daniels to the witness stand.

The public gallery waited, hushed in anticipation.

Dr Daniel, began Charles Matthews, *did you also examine my client at the police station in Wareham?*

Yes, I did. His pulse was at 140. He was very excited and I thought that he might be suffering from Delirium Tremens.

And what precisely is Delirium Tremens, Doctor Daniel?

It is a rapid onset of hallucination, confusion, twitching, irritability, and shaking, which is usually brought about by a withdrawal from alcohol.

Thank you, Doctor.

Charles Matthews now changed tack, producing a large leather volume, which he opened, with no small degree of theatre:

I have here a learned work by Dr Spencer Taylor, entitled 'Taylor's Medical Jurisprudence', in which the good doctor describes the commonality of hereditary insanity and homicidal mania. Are you familiar with this work and with its conclusions, Dr Daniel?

Yes.

And would you agree with Dr Taylor's conclusion that insanity is pre-disposed?

There is some accuracy in his remarks, admitted Dr Daniel.

And might my client's twitching and irritability be a result of insanity?

Yes, a twitching of the face and a change of manner might also be indicators of insanity.

Thank you, Doctor. No further questions.

However, Charles Matthews's attempt to lean the Grand Jury towards a verdict of insanity were dealt a blow by the next two witnesses to testify.

At the request of Mr Justice Lopes, Mr WE Good, the Dorset County Prison surgeon, had met with the prisoner on several occasions since his arrest:

Mr Good, began Charles Matthews, *you have attended the prisoner repeatedly I understand? What is your opinion of him?*

I have had conversations with him on ordinary matters and he has given rational answers. He has spoken to me about his family, his business, and his mode of life. He has always given reasonable answers. I have not the slightest reason to believe that he is suffering from a delusion of any kind or that he is in any way insane. He is, in my opinion, perfectly sane.

Mr Justice Lopes interjected with a question of his own, *Do you think he was capable of knowing what he did?*

He is perfectly sane.

Somewhat flustered, Charles Matthews attempted to question the validity of Mr Good's testimony, *You do not think the prisoner's mind is unhinged? Yet, have you not noticed his face constantly twitching; or that he cannot look anyone in the face? Is he not a man likely to become excited at the smallest provocation?*

I put it to him plainly in conversation that I thought there was little chance of his life being spared, and he displayed no extraordinary excitement.

Charles Matthews had a little more luck with his next witness, Captain Frederick Frith (the Governor of Dorchester Prison), who had also spoken to Henry Wright on several occasions since his arrest:

I had many conversations with the prisoner during his time on remand, Captain Frith began, *I believed him to be sane but peculiar.*

What do you mean by peculiar, Captain Frith?'

He found it perfectly impossible to fix his eyes on me while I was talking to him, and I noticed a twitching and a suppressed irritability. In fact, I was so taken by it, I directed the surgeon to watch over him.

The Rev HP Raikes, the prison chaplain, was next to take his place on the witness stand:

I have had the opportunity of seeing the prisoner on several occasions. His answers to me were at times rational and at other times incoherent and wandering. He scarcely knew what he was talking about. Last Monday I spoke to him about the library book he was reading, and he said he did not like it as well as the last one. When I asked him why, he said he did not know. He spoke once or twice about the case. but I thought that he did not speak rationally. He might first say one thing then contradict himself. I asked him if he had any defence and he replied 'Oh no! I don't care about that'.

Hoping that he had repaired the damage, Charles Matthews began to reveal Henry Wright's past to the jury. Joseph Rockwell, his next witness, stated for the court that he had known the prisoner since his birth in Ramsgate more than thirty years ago:

I knew his mother before he was born, and during the time she was pregnant her mind was very much deranged. She would sometimes roam about the fields for a part of the day and night. After he was born, his mother tried to destroy herself three times. She had a keeper, who watched her for eight or nine months, and was paid for by the family because she was so bad. She was then removed to Camberwell Lunatic Asylum and remained there for three years.

And did she recover, Mr Rockwell?

No, sir. She became worse again, and they sent her to the lunatic ward of the workhouse, where she died. Both his mother's parents also died in lunatic asylums.

And what about my client himself?

He had never been right since he was a boy. He was known in Ramsgate as 'Mad Joe' When I saw the story of his arrest in the local paper, I communicated with the police. I knew he was not right in the head.

The next witness, Alfred Bowler, a cook from Ramsgate, explained to the court that he had employed the prisoner:

When he was a lad, I employed him as a baker's assistant. He was always peculiar, and I had to discharge him. I never thought he was sane.

When was the last time you saw him, Mr Bowler?, enquired Charles Matthews.

I saw him a year ago, in June 1881, sir. I thought him unaltered since I first knew him.

Very well, thank you, Mr Rockwell.

The final witness for the defence was Henry Wright's elder brother, Daniel Kingsford:

Mr Kingsford, asked Charles Matthews, *were you aware that my client had taken to calling himself Henry Wright?*

No sir, I was not.

That is understandable. Can you now please tell the court something of your brother's background.

He is my youngest brother, sir. He had three brothers and two sisters, but he was the youngest. After he was born, his mother died in an asylum, as also did his grandfather and grandmother. He was always eccentric and very changeable, and his brain wandered.

With his final witness finished, Charles Matthews read out a statement from Henry Wright, as was the custom during Victorian trials. It was felt that the defendant might well prejudice their own case if they were allowed to be subjected to cross-examination during their trial. Henry Wright's statement – which was surely one of the shortest ever to be read out at a Victorian trial - simply stated, *I did it because he would not share his food and drink.*

That ended the case for the defence. The prosecution gave their summation for the Crown, reminding the jury of the prisoner's confession following his arrest. In addition, it was pointed out that although the defence had shown their client's historic mental state and family background, that did not mean he was necessarily insane at the time of the murder.

It was now time for Charles Matthews's summation for the defence. He would need to overcome the apparent confession given by his client at the police station, and his obvious indifference to the crime. Matthews would have to be at his eloquent best:

Gentleman of the jury, the task which has been imposed on you is the most important one that can fall to mortals to discharge, because upon your judgement depends the salvation or the sacrifice of a fellow creature's life. It is impossible to overestimate the importance of this issue. The question you have now to determine is whether the crime charged to the account of the prisoner was one for which he should die, or, whether in the evidence before you, you can see sufficient to convince yourselves that, at the time he committed the act complained of, he was not in the possession of his senses. That is the only question.

All I have endeavoured to elicit from witnesses is whether upon that day the unhappy man in the dock was so excited with drink - so excited that he was refused more drink at the Castle Inn by Mr Miller. I believe that when you come to see the evidence by the light thrown upon it by the condition of the prisoner, your decision will be a very different one to the one you first thought you might reach. Questions of fact should not trouble you much in this enquiry; what you have to decide is a much more difficult question than one of fact. It is a duty cast upon men who have, not to deduce inferences from fact, but who have to examine critically and with certainty, into the delicate organisation of the human mind. It is indeed to throw upon mortals the functions of the Most High.

Furthermore, that difficulty is enhanced a thousandfold by the man you now have to deal with - a being deranged, strange, and peculiar. Is it not impossible for human beings, such as we are, to look into such a mind as that of the man before you today, and say with certainty, knowing what turns upon that certainty, that at the time he committed this act there was intention to kill, and that the intention was fully developed.

Charles Matthews then reinforced his plea by reminding the jury that:

Dr Woodruffe Daniel has agreed that the taint of insanity is hereditary, passing from one generation to the next, and *that the prisoner himself from boyhood had been regarded strange, excitable, inconsequential, and unable to give his undivided attention to anything.*

He continued:

The important evidence of the prisoner's state of mind on the 29ᵗʰ of May this year is crucial. You must decide if the remarks of the governor and chaplain of the prison mean that you form the opinion that the prisoner was insane and unaccountable for his actions. If you waiver, I also remind you of the evidence of the prison surgeon, in which he remarked that the prisoner remained callous and indifferent when told he would probably be hanged for his crime. Does this not prove he was not in his right senses?

Stopping to draw breath for the briefest of moments, Charles Matthews continued, firstly choosing the highly unusual tactic of praising the prosecution:

And now, my task is done; my heart has been lightened by those who have conducted the prosecution, for it was spoken by honest men who asked, not for the fantastic theories of doctors, nor upon the fantastic theories which come from persons who have given insanity as their special study, but, instead, upon the reliable testimony of witnesses who surely were not mistaken when they stated that the prisoner was not responsible when he committed this crime.

Pausing again, this time to allow the jury to grasp the seriousness of the decision they were about to make, he then resumed his summation:

You will shortly have to consider whether the life of this man should be taken or whether it should be spared. Most earnest, most sorry is your duty, but in the consideration of it, I am quite sure that you will not forget that what is asked of you is not this man's freedom, but his existence. I pray to you for this man's life - a priceless gift to one who stands upon the very precipice of his fate.

Deal with him as mercifully as you can, so that you do not condemn him for the remainder of his life to the stigma of the Lazar house (a home for those with infectious diseases), where – and I use the words of the great Lord Byron from his work, 'The Lament of Tasso':

> *In this vast Lazar-house of many woes? Where laughter is not mirth, nor thought the mind, Nor words a language, nor ev'n men mankind; Where cries reply to curses, shrieks to blows. And each is tortured in his separate hell.*

Charles Matthews sat down to rapturous applause from the public gallery, which Justice Lopes was forced to suppress, before he could sum up the case for the benefit of the jury:

Your duty, he began, *is the most solemn any human being could be called upon to perform, but you must not allow the momentous nature of that duty to interfere with its proper discharge. Although solemn as your duty now is, it has been greatly lightened, and assisted by the man who has just sat down – the Counsel for the defence. He has freely tendered his services on behalf of the prisoner at the bar, and he has conducted the case for him with ability and eloquence. We are much indebted to him. Members of the jury, the only question you have to consider is the man's mental condition at the time he committed the act. Please now retire and consider your verdict.*

The jury duly retired.

The *Dorset County Chronicle* would later describe Henry Wright's demeanour during the proceedings:

The prisoner remained almost unchanged during the trial, which lasted four hours. Seated in corner of the dock, with his drowsy, unanimated eyes fixed upon the floor, he apparently felt not the slightest interest in the important issue being determined with much care around him. To all appearances, he paid but little heed to the damning evidence of his heinous crime, and it was not until his own friends appeared in the witness box - his eldest brother, his employer when a lad, and Mr Rockwell, the old friend of his family that his manner changed. Old memories seemed to be awakened in his dull brain, a drooping affection appeared to be revived in his hard heart, there was still a spark of humanity left in him. It seemed too much for him - the tears would come, and for a moment or two he buried his face in his handkerchief and wept bitterly. Then his callousness re-appeared, and remained unmoved to the end of the trial, unmoved and indifferent even during the eloquent appeal made on his behalf by his learned advocate, and unchanged, even when at last the case was over, and the jury had returned their verdict.

Henry Wright did not have long to wait. The jury returned just ten minutes later. When asked if they had reached a verdict, Mr Freeman from Weymouth, the jury spokesman, answered,

We find the prisoner guilty, but we do not consider he was responsible for his act.

Justice Lopes replied: *Then that is a verdict of not guilty on the grounds of insanity. The prisoner will be detained during Her Majesty's pleasure.*

Henry Wright was then removed and returned to his prison cell in Dorchester. However, he did not remain there for long. A recommendation was made that he be transferred into, 'Strict and secure custody at Broadmoor Criminal Lunatic Asylum in Berkshire, until Her Majesty's pleasure concerning him be known.'

He was never to enjoy 'Her Majesty's pleasure'. Henry Wright lived out the remainder of his life incarcerated at Broadmoor, before passing away in 1908 at the age of 59.

Little is known of Dennis Riley. During his trial, it was mentioned that his name was almost certainly an alias. He was buried in a pauper's grave, alongside the beggar's certificate which had been among the articles found in his possession at the time of the murder. The *Vagrancy Act 1824* dictated that any beggar or pedlar found 'placing himself or herself in any public place to beg or gather alms shall be deemed an idle and disorderly person, and liable to imprisonment.

The beggar's certificate simply read, *Dennis Riley, Beggar, 5' 6", Dark Hair, dark eyes.*

THE CHARMOUTH
CHURCH MYSTERY

The ill-judged execution of the well-judged plan
Thomas Hardy, *Tess of the D'Urbervilles*

Thomas Hardy drew inspiration for many of the people
and plots in his Wessex novels and short stories from the
colourful characters he observed in the county or read
about in the Dorset newspapers. Indeed, he carefully
pasted newspaper cuttings into several notebooks which are
now kept in the Dorset County archives. It is tempting to
think that the following tale may have inspired some of the
minor characters and rural subplots that helped him create
such a vivid portrayal of Wessex life in the Victorian era.

The parish church of St Andrew's in Charmouth had
been constructed in 1835, on the site of a much older
building, at the considerable cost of £3,098 (almost
£500,000 today). Probably due to a family connection in
the area, the famous architect Charles Fowler was chosen
to design and build the new church. Fowler, a famous and
highly respected designer, had become well-known for his
architectural achievements such as Covent Garden Market
and Hungerford Market in London and the church of St
John the Evangelist in Hyde Park.

Partly as a result of the ornate and welcoming new church, the congregation increased under Rev. Edward Breton, as did the need for increased burial space. By the early 1860s plans were underway to extend the front of the churchyard at St Andrew's, by the purchase and demolition of two old and unsightly buildings in The Street. More money would need to be raised to finance this endeavour; along with the need to collect extra funds from the weekly services. Staff numbers were increasing; there was a parish clerk, sexton and cleaner to pay. Yet, despite the increasing congregation, the receipts from the church contribution box seemed to worsen every week. The proceeds from these contributions were used to pay various sundry church costs, as well as for distribution among several deserving causes as part of the Parish Poor Relief scheme.

In May 1863 an urgent meeting was called to discuss this unexplained dip in the generosity of Charmouth's townsfolk. Many had given generously or worked hard to raise funds during the construction of the church in 1835. Now the contributions to the church had dwindled to just a few 'coppers'. It seemed that the residents of Charmouth had stopped donating any silver coins. The box no longer contained any half-crowns, shilling pieces, or even sixpences.

Had the townsfolk fallen out of love with the church; had the Minister Edward Breton upset his flock? Surely not, it was generally thought. He was a well-respected 59-year-old, with an eminently suitable family, and had already been Rector at St Andrew's for two decades. Yet something was clearly amiss. Questions were asked. Those who attended the church regularly undoubtedly resented the

directness of the accusations, however they claimed that
their contributions had not reduced. Something was clearly
amiss at St Andrew's Church. The unpleasant truth would
now need to be addressed. Was someone in Charmouth
committing 'Sacrilege at Charmouth', as the Dorset
County Chronicle' would label it, stealing from the church?

Parish clerk Digory Gordge and his nephew Job Gordge,
the church sexton, were questioned regarding the security
arrangements at St Andrew's. Job Gordge verified that,
together with his wife Ann who cleaned the church, that
they were the last two people to leave the building in the
evenings. Job confirmed that the offertory box was always
locked with the key which had been entrusted to him,
and that the belfry door was also locked before they left.
This was confirmed by his uncle, Digory Gordge, who
often opened the building in the mornings. On entering
the church there appeared to be no sign of a break in,
and nothing seemed to have been disturbed. However,
Rector Edward Breton was not satisfied. Either the
whole congregation was engaged in a bizarre town-wide
conspiracy, or the truth lay closer to home. He decided to
undertake an investigation of his own.

On 18th May 1863 Rev Breton summoned Andrew Tucker,
his churchwarden. Tucker also happened to be a local
solicitor and enjoyed a position of trust and respect within
the town. In the nineteenth century the crime of theft was
considered more serious than crimes such as assault or
public brawling. While the offence of a man striking his
wife, or of fighting in a public house might be attributed
(or even excused by) the consumption of excess alcohol,
or the nagging of an unsympathetic spouse, the offence

of thieving was most certainly not. In an age when most business and commerce relied on an element of trust, punishments for theft were deliberately punitive.

Mr Tucker and Rev Breton agreed that the church box must have been systematically robbed for a period of at least a month. Andrew Tucker did not take the matter lightly and immediately contacted Superintendent McHale of the newly formed Dorset County Constabulary. McHale then contacted PC Hawker, the local Charmouth constable, and the three men set in place an imaginative 'sting' operation.

The solicitor was joined by the two police officers for a secret meeting on the night of Saturday 23rd May at The Cottage, his home in The Street (now known as Albury House). By candlelight, and with McHale and PC Hawker as witnesses, Tucker took his pocket-knife and carefully etched a cross on the tail side of one half-crown, two one-shilling pieces, and two sixpence pieces. The amount, today's equivalent of approximately £40, was thought sufficient to tempt even the pettiest of thieves. Then, under cover of darkness, Tucker and Hawker entered the church and carefully placed the marked silver coins into the offertory box. It was then simply a matter of watching and waiting. Andrew Tucker kept a watchful eye on St Andrew's from The Street outside during the day; whilst at night Rev. Breton listened carefully from the Rectory at the rear of the church for the sound of the break in. Meanwhile, PC Hawker maintained a watching brief while patrolling the town.

However, despite the trio's best efforts, a fortnight passed without incident. Job Gordge and his wife, Ann, continued to lock up the church each evening. There were no signs of any disturbance and both the building, and the contribution box remained undisturbed. In fact, nothing seemed out of place at all. On the night of Saturday 6th June, after Job Gordge had locked up for the evening, Tucker and Hawker decided to meet again at St Andrew's. The two men carefully opened the offertory box to discover to their surprise that the silver coins they had placed inside two weeks previously had all disappeared. Rev. Breton assured the two men that he had not opened the box since their subterfuge was set in motion a fortnight earlier. The field of suspects was narrowing.

Tucker and Hawker decided to repeat the trap. However, on this occasion, the two men held a series of meetings with local shop and innkeepers in Charmouth, who were warned to keep a close eye on any silver coins that crossed their counters. Each shopkeeper was then sworn to secrecy. Would the thief be audacious – or foolish – enough to try and pass the marked coins so close to the scene of the crime? Only time would tell.

Among the local shopkeepers visited were John Carter the postmaster and village grocer, John Hodges the butcher, and George Holly from the Coach and Horses Inn. Although these premises were all close to the church, they served the majority of the townsfolk and seemed to be the most probable locations in which the coins might be used by the elusive thief.

And so, on Sunday 7th June, Andrew Tucker and PC Hawker set the second phase of their careful plan into motion. Two distinctive coins were chosen. A Queen Victoria half-sovereign and a one-shilling piece were selected. Both coins were still shiny and easily recognisable, and both were dated '1859'. Andrew Tucker once again took his pocket-knife and meticulously etched a distinctive cross pattern underneath the crown on the tail side of the coins. Early the following morning, the two men proceeded to the empty church and carefully placed the coins inside the contribution box; then withdrew quietly to await the result of their endeavours.

On this occasion they would not have long to wait.

Andrew Tucker would later describe the events of the 8th June, at a specially convened magistrate's hearing:

On Monday, the 8th of June, I placed the half-sovereign and shilling, so marked, into the box. Yesterday, Job Gordge, his daughter, and his wife, were in the church, cleaning out. After they left to go to dinner, about half-past one o'clock, I went into the church, and opened the box, and there found the half-sovereign and shilling still untouched.

I noticed that the half-sovereign was the same one that I had marked and placed in the box earlier. On going back into the church, that same night, about quarter past nine, after the church had been locked up by Job Gordge, who is the sexton, and also keeps the key of the belfry door, I again opened the box. This time I discovered the half-sovereign and shilling had been abstracted. I immediately went for PC Hawker and informed him of what had occurred. I accompanied the police-constable to Job Gordge's house, and there we found the half-sovereign, now produced, which is the same one I marked and placed the box.

PC Hawker was also present at the magistrate's hearing and added:

Mr Tucker, in my presence, marked a half-crown, two one shilling pieces, and two sixpences, which were then placed in the poor-box by Mr Tucker. About a fortnight after, Mr Tucker informed me the money was gone. On Sunday, the 7th inst., I saw Mr Tucker mark a half-sovereign with a cross on the tail side, and also a shilling. From information received from Mr. Tucker, on the 17th inst., I went to the house of Job Gordge and I apprehended the prisoner. On searching his house, his wife produced some money, from a tin in the parlour, and amongst it, was the half-sovereign now produced here, and which is the same I saw him mark and put in the box.

It seemed a straightforward case to the local magistrate, and he recommended that the case was put forward to the Quarter Assizes at Dorchester, which were traditionally convened on the last day of each quarter (in this case, 30th June 1863).

Job Gordge was not permitted to speak, but was granted bail, before being committed to trial.

To the residents of Charmouth, it seemed a straight-forward case. The sin of stealing from the church was unsurprisingly deemed an egregious one and it is likely that Job Gordge would not have garnered much sympathy.

The Gordge family, however, were a large and well-known family in the town. Digory Gordge, Job's uncle, had been parish clerk for many years and, prior to his death in 1861, had doubtless recommended his nephew for the role of sexton at St Andrew's. In turn, Digory Gordge's father and grandfather (who had also been named Digory), had both been previous clerks to the parish. However, it appears that the family's record was not without blemish, as Digory Gordge's grandfather had been arrested and charged for smuggling in 1765. This incident was recorded in the vestry minutes at the time, along with a resolution among those present at the meeting to pay for his defence. It seems that there was some sympathy among church officials for the plight of local smugglers.

Although the church had largely ignored and tolerated the previous smuggling activities of Digory Gordge, it was no doubt conscious of the damage to its reputation caused by such scandals. St Andrew's reputation had previously suffered, due to the activities of a notorious former incumbent as Rector. The Rev John Audain had become Minister at Charmouth in 1783 at the age of just 18. He had only recently been ordained and his surprising appointment was largely due to his close relationship with the Lord of the manor at the time, Francis Phipps Henvill. Audain, however, spent little time in Charmouth, preferring to spend time in his family's home in the West Indies, engaged in the slave trade. His exploits became legendary, and were recorded in 1825 by Henry Nelson Coleridge (nephew and editor for Samuel Coleridge):

His appearance was fine, gentle and venerable, and he supplemented his stipend as Rector of Charmouth by owning a small privateer. His schooner was captured, while smuggling negroes to Guadeloupe, by another vessel from the isle of Nevis. The Parson then went to Nevis, posted his rival's name on the Courthouse door, and stood guard there for three days in the hope that the man would come and challenge him to a duel. He had fought thirteen duels in his life, and on one occasion, while waiting for the seconds to reload, he went up to his opponent, suggested 'just a little something to fill the time, good sir' and knocked him flat with his fist!

Clearly there was little appetite for any more scandal among the congregation at St Andrew's and consequently the trial of Job Gordge at Dorchester Assizes seems to have been a curious one.

Job Gordge was charged with 'Larceny and receiving whilst employed as a sexton', to which he pleaded 'not guilty'. Although in 1863 a defendant was not permitted to speak in his own defence, a statement was read out on his behalf:

I received the sovereign some time ago from Mr John Carter, the postmaster, of Charmouth, and upon the same day changed it at Mr Holly's, the Coach and Horses Inn, and received, in part change, the half-sovereign found in my house.

Despite the fact that he clearly could not have received the sovereign coin *some time ago*, as Andrew Tucker had only placed it in the church collection box on 7th June, and the near impossibility that both marked coins would happen to end up in his possession both simultaneously and by coincidence, Job Gordge was found not guilty of theft and released without charge. Perhaps the church, wishing to avoid any further scandal, also paid for Job Gordge's defence or asserted some influence over the proceedings?

The Gordge family were once a large and colourful dynasty within the town of Charmouth. Five brothers were recorded in the town during the late 1700s, all of whom seem to have had large families of between ten and fifteen children. The name Gordge probably derives from the Middle English 'gorger' and old French 'gorgiere' - a maker of throat armour and later a maker of cloths and wimples designed to cover the neck.

Before becoming sexton at the church, Job Gordge had been employed as an agricultural labourer on a nearby farm. Unfortunately, he gained an unwanted reputation for being unreliable, drinking heavily, and for regularly being late for work. This culminated in his dismissal in 1859, and a drunken brawl in The Coach and Horses public house, resulting in a court appearance and a sentence of two months hard labour at Dorchester Jail. His uncle, Digory Gordge, no doubt secured his nephew the role of church sexton upon his release.

There may have been little sympathy for Job Gordge's alleged crime in Charmouth, however, there was certainly much compassion for his wife Ann and their family of ten children. Sadly, Job Gordge did not see the error of his ways and continued drinking heavily, appearing in court once more in 1864. He died just two years later at the age of only 36.

Members of the Gordge family may have also been involved in the Chartist movement during the 1840s. The movement, which spread rapidly to Dorset and

other rural areas from its roots in London, sought to gain
further political rights and influence for the working classes
following the failure of the 1832 Reform Act to address
this. Many workers were persecuted for their support in
this struggle, such as George Loveless and the Tolpuddle
Martyrs, and William Henry Gordge, yet another uncle of
Job's. William Henry Gordge was transported to Australia
for seven years in 1818, for his part in a robbery from a
Charmouth merchant. After being pardoned, he returned
to Charmouth, before eventually settling in Swansea
following yet another prison sentence for theft at the
Swansea House of Corrections.

So, it seems that Job Gordge was not the only black sheep
in the Gordge family.

Curiously, although St Andrew's Church and its adjoining
churchyard are liberally sprinkled with memorials to the
prolific Gordge family, which can still be viewed, there are
no descendants still remaining in the town.

It is tempting, nevertheless, to think that Thomas Hardy
may have happened upon the stories of Digory Gordge
and Job Gordge during his research; and been influenced
by their stories when creating some of his colourful rural
characters, such as Diggory Venn in *Return of the Native*, and
Abel Whittle in *The Mayor of Casterbridge*.

St Andrew's also features elsewhere in this book. A
monument to the Galpin family, mentioned in the chapter,
The Bridport Bread Riots, can be found at the church,
although Thomas Carter Galpin is buried at Highgate
Cemetery in London.

THE CRY FROM THE GRAVE
(PART ONE)

Is it conceivable that a supernatural cry from the grave may have alerted the authorities to the possibility of an unknown murder? There is seemingly well documented evidence that, in the quiet village of Beaminster in June 1728, an improbable chain of events may have prevented a glaring injustice from being buried forever. The sudden appearance of a ghostly apparition transformed the tragic death of a schoolboy from one of supposed ill health, to one of murder.

Young John Daniel's story is a heart-breaking one, ending in a tragic death. However, just a few weeks after his demise, a chilling twist in the tale would create a legend that cannot be fully explained, even today.

Yet even before his mysterious death, his short life had been a tragic one.

Isaac Daniel married Hannah Collins in Lyme Regis during October 1712. Isaac was a manorial tenant farmer with a valuable smallholding for which he had secured what was then referred to as a 'Lord's Lease' or a 'Lifeholder's Copyhold Lease', from the manor of Beaminster Prima. For the payment of a considerable sum in advance, the tenant was entitled to a lifelong lease on his property at a low annual rent (far less than the actual annual rental value of the land). In addition, prior to the leaseholder' death, he was able to nominate his immediate dependant, or dependants, to become the subsequent tenant of the land, upon his death. This right, known as 'Lord's next tenant', offered considerable financial security for a widowed family and might often turn a comparatively short leasehold into a far longer one, should the descendants of the original tenant live for a considerable time. The value of Isaac Daniel's smallholding was estimated to be around £300 at that time, a sizeable sum equivalent to approximately £100,000 today.

Hannah Daniel fell pregnant in early 1714 and the couple's first son, John, was born in the autumn. Sadly, it seems likely that Hannah must have endured a difficult pregnancy and childbirth, as she passed away shortly afterwards and was buried at St Mary's Church in Beaminster on 15th October. John Daniel would grow up never knowing his mother. However, both Hannah Daniel and St Mary's Church would later play a dramatic part in the story.

Isaac Daniel brought up his young son, with the help of the family's servant Elizabeth Stodgell, at the Daniel family home on the corner of Hogshill Street and Shadrack Street. The house is now known as Daniel's House, although the original structure was severely damaged during a serious fire in 1781, and has since been largely rebuilt and extended.

A relationship clearly blossomed between the widower, Isaac Daniel, and his female servant, as the couple married

in February 1717 and soon after had a son of their own,
Isaac junior. Both boys were enrolled at Beaminster
School, under the stewardship of headmaster John Guppy.
With no official school building, Beaminster School was
housed in the gallery of St Mary's Church, in the south-

eastern corner of the
building and reached via
an outside stairway from
the churchyard. The late
medieval church with its
striking Gothic tower and
ornate carving provided
a worthy backdrop to the
remarkable events that
were to follow.

The years passed without incident, until August 1726 when
John Daniel had reached the age of twelve. His father
rapidly became seriously ill. Too sick and weak to write a
formal will, he summoned three witnesses in order that he
might formally exercise his rights of tenancy and decree
that his smallholding could be passed legally to his children.
This form of declaration, known as a nuncupative will,
was commonly used in cases where a very sick person was
too feeble, or did not have sufficient time left, to construct
a formally written will. Amendments to the *Statute of Wills
Act* in 1661 had made allowance for a dying man to divide
his property between more than one child (rather than his
estate being automatically inherited by the eldest sibling).
As was legally required, three witnesses were summoned to
Isaac's deathbed, where the dying man's final wishes were
duly recorded and witnessed; to be enacted following his
passing.

Isaac Daniel left his worldly possessions to his wife, Elizabeth, and to each of the sons the sum of five shillings. In addition, John was granted one acre of arable land and five acres of pasture, John's younger half-brother, Isaac junior, received a half-acre of arable and eight acres of pasture (although, under the terms of the *Statute of Wills Act*, neither child could receive their inheritance until their fourteenth birthdays).

Unfortunately, John's anticipated succession to his combined smallholding of six acres was to end in tragedy. Just a few months prior to his fourteenth birthday (according to a contemporary and anonymous handwritten account):

John, happening to be somewhat infirm, whither by the importunity or love of fear of his stepmother, or what other motive prevailed on him is not known, nominated his said stepmother to be the Lord's next tenant to said estate after him.

It appears that, in a similar vein to his father, John realised the importance of exercising his right to appoint a 'Lord's next tenant' as a contingency; in the event that something might happen to him.

He continued his studies at Beaminster School and tended to the animals and land, according to his stepmother's wishes. One dry and warm day in late May 1728, in what had been an otherwise wet start to the summer, John was instructed by his stepmother, Elizabeth, to tend the family's cows in the fields behind their home.

However, as afternoon became evening, and then evening became night, John failed to return. Nevertheless, Elizabeth

Daniel does not appear to have been unduly concerned since, according to the same handwritten document, she did not initiate a search of any kind for her stepson until the following morning.

The Daniel family was a long established one in Beaminster, and well known among the small community. Yet, no one in the village remembered witnessing John that night. One of the older boys at the school, he was also known to be sporting a distinctive white cloth or rag wrapped around his right hand. According to his stepmother, John's hand had 'gone lame', probably resulting from a fall or a knock suffered during one of the fits or seizures from which his mother claimed he suffered, and that he had wrapped the piece of white material around his hand four or five days prior to his death.

It was the beginning of summer, offering the villagers long hours of daylight to utilise in their search for the missing boy. The field close to the Daniel's home seemed the obvious place to begin the quest, since John had been sent there by his stepmother to feed the cattle. Tragically, it would not be long before the body of the boy was discovered lying on a small island of gravel and sand created in a flowing stream which wound its way through part of the field. Although John's body was discovered comparatively close to his home (approximately 220 yards away), it was in an unusual location; being neither at a point at which he was likely to have been tending the cattle, nor on his logical route to or from the family's cottage. Perhaps whilst suffering one of the dramatic seizures or fits, as described by his stepmother, John had wandered blindly, before eventually collapsing.

The handwritten contemporary account described the body as lying in a 'very odd posture' and exhibiting 'several black spots around his neck, and on his breast and belly', which seemed to be 'tokens of violence.' The revelation of this alarming discovery caused the writer of the anonymous account to speculate further regarding:

The improbability of his voluntarily going to the place where he was found dead', together with a 'great suspicion in the child's relations and neighbourhood that he had been murdered, occasioned no small stir amongst the people.

Despite his death being both a highly unusual and sudden one, especially considering the victim's slender years, no official inquest or inquiry was held, and John Daniel was subsequently buried in St Mary's churchyard just a few days later, on Saturday 1ˢᵗ June. Elizabeth Daniel's explanation that her stepson was 'subject to fits', apparently assuaged the suspicions of locals and negated any such formality. In 1728, no official autopsy, doctor's certificate or registration was legally required. Nevertheless, births, deaths and marriages were expected to be entered in local parish records. This was by no means a legal formality, however; meaning that many deaths were never recorded. During the eighteenth-century these records were not coordinated nationally, and it would be more than a century later until an accurate national register was proposed, under the terms of the *Births and Deaths Registration Act 1836.* Even then, this did not yet require a cause of death to be certified by a doctor. In fact, it was not until a tightening of the act in 1874 that a death certificate became a legal requirement; at which point an immediate burial was expected. This urgency had the effect of allowing many a suspicious death to go undetected.

Returning to 1728, with no official evidentiary records surrounding John's cause of death required, and no inquiry, it seems that any proof of foul play in the death of John Daniels was literally 'dead and buried'. If, indeed, John had actually been murdered, his killer could now breathe a little easier.

However, the ghostly spirit of John clearly had other ideas.

On Saturday 22nd June, four weeks after John's death, a macabre incident would take place at St Mary's Church, resulting in an extraordinary chain of events and a remarkable disclosure.

The strange happenings of 22nd June were later described at the Coroner's Inquest by a fellow senior pupil at Beaminster School, David Harbin, and outlined once more in a 1774 edition of the respected journal, the *Gentleman's Magazine* under the heading:

The following very singular story comes well authenticated

 Both accounts were independently obtained, yet strikingly similar. David Harbin's statement read as follows:

I hereby testify that I am a true and honest witness to the events of the 22nd day of June, 1728. I am one of twenty boys benefiting from the charity of our much-missed benefactor, the late Mrs Tucker, whose will has provided for us the sum of £20 a year, derived from the income of her farm at South Mapperton. A portion of the fund provides for a schoolmaster, one who has been most effective in teaching me to read and write — not to mention, taking care to develop my manners; though his tendency to catechise me (instruct someone in principles of the Christian religion) *in a most peculiar manner is certainly unprecedented, but one that I have no wish to make complaint of.*

We are schooled in the upper room of an annex attached to the southwest corner of St. Mary's Church, which is the location of the events I hereby describe.

For those unaware of the long-held customs and traditions of our school, the closure of the schoolroom follows a rather tiresome procedure: every Saturday after studies (at 12pm), *the key of the room is returned to the clerk of the parish by one or the other of the schoolboys. In recent months, that duty has fallen upon myself.*

On the Saturday in question, I had handed the key over as usual, then followed my master to dismiss the boys. However, having overseen their passage from the church one half hour earlier, I noticed, with some embarrassment, that eight of the boys remained, loitering within the churchyard where they were involved in a game of ball. It was just about noon. I questioned the boys regarding their reasons for staying — the lads appeared somewhat nervous — and I was soon informed that they were waiting for four of their number who had re-entered the school in search of old pens.

With this, I felt it important to ascertain if there was any impropriety in their aforementioned activity. Walking towards the church, I was startled to hear much commotion; the four boys having emerged from the church appearing shaken and drawn. After recovering their breaths — they had obviously been running at quite a speed — they revealed the source of their distress: they had each been frightened by a sharp, metallic sound emanating from the chancel, something they described as resembling the repeated striking of a brass pan. The four immediately ran to their friends in the churchyard and told them of it. After much searching for rationality, they came to the conclusion that someone, quite probably a fellow pupil, had secreted himself inside the church in order to frighten them; and deciding upon this, I joined their number in returning to the school to discover the boy's identity; but our search was in vain, for there was not a soul hiding within.

As the boys returned to their sport (and I to my studies) via the worn steps that ran rigidly into the churchyard, we all heard a second burst of discordance, undoubtedly louder than the first for it had broken through the walls of the church. Terrified at this, we ran round the church, and when at the west door, we heard what seemed to be the sound of someone preaching, soon followed by another sound, that of a congregation singing psalms. Both of these noises lasted but a short time.

With the impetuosity of youth, unencumbered by self-doubt, the lads soon resumed their sport, whilst I remained close to the church. After a short time, one of them went into the school to retrieve his book; but seconds after the boy's entrance, we heard a most appalling shriek, followed by a moment of whimpering. What this boy revealed, after he had returned to the churchyard as distraught as those who had gone in search of pens, was a most chilling experience: when passing through the nave, he had seen a coffin lying on one of the benches, only about six feet away. Astonishing, as there had not been a funeral that morning; nor would there be one tomorrow.

Alarmed by such a solemn statement, I took to the door of the church, whereupon a throng of twelve surrounded me, and as God is my witness I saw with my own eyes the scene previously described to me; a coffin sat upon a distant bench, with its lid open, and there, worse still, the apparition of John Daniel, who had been dead some weeks, sitting at some distance from the coffin, near to the chancel. I am now aware that only six of us were witness to the said phantom, and it is my conjecture that all did not see the apparition because the door was so narrow that we could not all approach it together. The first who knew it to be the spectre of our deceased schoolfellow was Isaac, Daniel's half-brother, and he, on seeing it, cried out, 'There sits our John, with just such a coat on as I have - (in the lifetime of the deceased boy the half-brothers were usually clothed alike), - with a pen in his hand, and a book before him, and a coffin by him. I'll throw a stone at him.' The other boys attempted to stop him, but he threw the stone, as he did so saying, 'Take it Johnnie!' upon which the phantom immediately disappeared.

The immense furore this created in Beaminster can only be imagined. David Harbin continued:

Despite our tender ages, ranging between eight and twelve, we were all magisterially examined by Colonel Broadrepp (the local Justice of the Peace), *and all agreed in what we had seen, even to the hinges of the coffin; whilst our descriptions of the coffin tallied exactly with that the deceased boy had been buried in. One of the lads, Samuel Coombe, who saw the apparition, was not quite twelve years of age, and was a quiet dispassionate lad for his age; he enrolled in the school after the deceased boy had left it and had never seen Daniel in his lifetime. The boy, on examination, gave such a vivid account of the deceased, and took especial notice of one thing about the spectre which the other boys had not mentioned, and that was, the body had a white cloth bound round one of its hands.*

Following the appearance of the supposed ghost of John Daniel, a public outcry ensued. The large number of witnesses to this apparent spectre at St Mary's Church seemed to be significant. Embers of local suspicion were ignited, eventually leading Colonel Broadrepp from Mapperton Manor to order an immediate investigation. He

requested the services of George Filliter, the Dorset coroner
and Town Clerk of Wareham, instructing him to order the
exhumation of the body (all witnesses and jurors present
at an eighteenth-century inquest were expected to view the
deceased's body).

The Minister of Beaminster Church, Peter Brice, was
instructed to arrange the exhumation, by means of a
Coroner's warrant and each of the Beaminster schoolboys
were questioned individually by Colonel Broadrepp. The
boys were not permitted to speak to each other before their
depositions were taken; yet each one gave a remarkably
similar version of the unsettling events.

It must be remembered that in 1728, any such supernatural
intervention, suggesting foul play, was far more likely to
be believed than perhaps it might be today. Arguably,
England (particularly rural England) lagged far behind
Europe in the era of enlightenment – the country had
still to adopt the Gregorian calendar and superstitious
folklore was revered and observed in almost every part of
daily rural life. Belief in witchcraft was still widespread
and, even though the printed media was still in its infancy
in 1728, chilling accounts of unexplained sightings such
as the ghost of Elizabeth Herle, accidently shot by her
husband at Dockacre House in Launceston, the vampires
of New Orleans, or the grey lady at The Crown Hotel in
Amersham, were a commonplace feature.

Events moved apace. On 5th July John Daniel's coffin was
exhumed from the burial ground. Two of the schoolboys,
who had both witnessed the ghostly vision inside the
church, were overheard remarking that the white gartering

tied to the handles of the boy's coffin matched that contained on the ghostly coffin they had witnessed at the church a few weeks earlier. Eerily, neither boy had actually attended John Daniel's funeral and therefore were not aware of the existence of this augmentation to the boy's coffin. Even more strangely, those present at John's burial on 1ˢᵗ June, including the church sexton, could not remember the presence of any such gartering tied to the handle of the coffin at the time of John's burial, although his stepmother swore it was present.

On the same day an instruction was sent to the Constables of Beaminster:

These are in his Majesties name to require you to warn four and twenty lawful men of the parish to be and appear before me George Filliter Gent, one of his Majesties Coroners of Dorsetshire, at the King's Arms in Beaminster in the said county to-morrow at seven of the clock in the morning to do what shall then and there be enjoined of them on behalf of his Majesty. And hereof you are not to fail and you are also to warn the persons hereunder named to be at the time and place foresaid. Witness my hand and seal, the 5ᵗʰ day of July in the first year of the reign of King George the 2ⁿᵈ AD 1728.

The warrant included the names of the twenty-four jurors (all men, and property owners aged between 21 and 70) and a further fourteen witnesses. Those present at the inquest included Elizabeth Daniel, Isaac junior, other members of the Daniel family, Edward Stodgell (a relative of John's stepmother), several neighbours, and the schoolboys who witnessed the apparition. While all of their names are not known, it is likely to have included Joseph Hooke, John Dunn, and Samuel Coombe.

The inquest into the cause of John Daniel's death opened at 7 o'clock on the morning of Saturday 6th July 1728 at the King's Arms in Beaminster, the body having been placed there the night before. The need to commence proceedings at such an early hour would become abundantly clear as the sun began to filter in through the windows, and the temperature soared. The coroner George Filliter, who had arrived the previous evening to ensure the safe conduct of the exhumed body, together with local surgeon (probably Henry Dunning of Bridge House), viewed the body along with the requisite number of witnesses.

Inquests during the 1700s were frequently held in public houses due to the lack of civic buildings in most towns and villages. The King's Arms in Fore Place (now The Square) was the most important building in Beaminster at that time. Despite its size and stature, however, it was of course entirely unsuitable for the performance of a meaningful and a hygienic autopsy; being cramped, poorly lit and inadequately ventilated. Indeed, the stench emanating from a six-week-old corpse, at the height of summer, and in such cramped and crowded surroundings, can only be imagined. Nevertheless, this did not deter the coroner, witnesses, and jury from completing their unpleasant task.

The sheer number of witnesses to the supernatural encounter at St Mary's Church seemed to add credibility to the likelihood of John Daniel having suffered an unlikely demise. Even David Harbin assumed that the ghostly vision indicated a violent end to John Daniel's life, and added the following to his statement:

It is only now that the full details of John Daniel's death have been revealed to me. His body had been found in such aberrant circumstances: lying in a field, a few hundred feet from his mother's house; and thereupon had been buried without an inquest, in event of his mother alleging that the lad had been prone to fits.

Yet the inquest and the story were both far from over. More striking evidence was to be revealed from the contemporary handwritten account, and the later article in the *Gentleman's Magazine*, which both added yet more detail of the experience suffered by the terrified schoolboys at St Mary's Church.

THE CRY FROM THE GRAVE
(PART TWO)

The inquest into the death of John Daniel continued at the King's Arms.

Whilst the contemporary handwritten document and the later *Gentleman's Magazine* account differ slightly, as each may well have reflected the experience of different witnesses, the similarities are remarkable, which seemed to add some validity to their claims.

Both documents mention the distinctive 'tingling noise', like a small bell being rung or a brass pan being struck. The *Gentleman's Magazine* article also mentions:

A second noise, as of a man going about in great boots. Terrified at that, they (the schoolboys) *ran round the church, and when at the belfry or west door they heard a third noise, like a minister preaching. Which was succeeded by another of a congregation singing psalms, both continued but a short time.*

The handwritten account suggests that only one of the boys present thought he 'heard the sound of someone following him', which caused him to turn around and notice that, 'at the farthest end of the school he saw an apparition of a white coffin with brass nails lying on a writing desk there. The group then, saw the apparition of

John Daniel sitting at a writing desk where he used to write when he was living.'

All the boys noticed that the ghostly vision was attired in his school clothing and hat, which cast a shadow across his face as he leaned over his desk. Also each boy distinctly remembered the white gartering attached to the coffin handles. At the time of the incident, it was possible, from the churchyard door (which opened inwards), to look up towards the far end of the gallery and view the spot at which the schoolboys claimed to have seen the coffin and the figure of John Daniel, apparently wearing school clothing and with a hat pulled down across his face. The staircase and gallery were removed later in the century when the school ceased to be held at the church.

According to the boys' accounts, after John Daniel's younger half-brother, Isaac junior, threw a stone towards the apparition it vanished, leaving the church clouded in a 'thick darkness' for a few minutes, before normality returned.

The inquest continued. Depositions were also taken by Colonel Broadrepp from two local women, both were neighbours of the Daniels, and both described as being 'of good repute'. Each woman testified to visiting John Daniel's mother two days after his body had been found, to pay their respects and to help prepare the deceased child for interment. They both swore under oath that John's body had a 'black list' (cloth) tied around its throat; which covered what seemed to be vivid bruising or markings on his neck.

The two neighbours continued, explaining how they had both helped John's grieving stepmother wrap the body in a two-piece shroud, one shroud placed underneath the victim, and one covering him from above. A local coffin maker, who had delivered the casket to the Daniels' home, confirmed the evidence of the two women. He also noticed the dramatic markings on the neck of the corpse as he lowered John's body into the coffin. It seems that the two-piece shroud failed to completely conceal the body, as a single shroud might have been expected to do:

The shroud, not being orderly put on the corpse, but cut in two pieces, one laid under and the other over it, gave an opportunity of observing it.

A single shroud was more commonly used, as traditionally it better protected the buried body from decomposition and from hungry animals. Why Elizabeth Daniel did not provide a single shroud, thus risking the markings on her stepson's neck being visible, is not immediately obvious, nor explained at the inquest. It does, however, appear to be hugely significant.

One of the two neighbours who had assisted in preparing the body for interment, also declared to Colonel Broadrepp that she had noticed a white cloth wrapped around John Daniel's hand, identical to the white cloth noticed by the schoolboy Samuel Coombe during the ghostly encounter at St Mary's Church.

It seems to have been assumed by Colonel Broadrepp and the jury at the King's Arms that the vivid trauma on the victim's neck, coupled with the apparent attempt to conceal it with a piece of black cloth, was evidence that a tourniquet had been applied to the boy's throat. The surgeon (referred to in the *Gentleman's Magazine* article by his charmingly archaic title 'the chirurgeon') was asked to express his opinion on the possibility of strangulation, to which he testified that he, 'could not or would not positively affirm to the jury that there was any dislocation of the neck.' Dislocations and fractures of the hyoid bone, cricoid and thyroid cartilages occur in well over half of all fatal strangulations. Even in 1728 the medical profession would have easily noticed such an injury post-mortem.

Nevertheless, despite the surgeon's reservations, the evidence of these two local women, coupled with that of the coffin maker, appears to have been crucial and the jury returned a verdict 'that the boy had been strangled.'

A coroner's inquest, of course, is not a trial. The guilt of person, or persons, unknown still needed to be proved in a court of law. This dramatic turn of events unsurprisingly sent shockwaves through the local community in Beaminster, yet there appears to be no record of any investigation, nor of anyone ever being brought to justice for John Daniel's murder. It seems that John's restless spirit had been roused in vain.

Nevertheless, the townsfolk harboured their own suspicions. The anonymous handwritten document published later in 1774 voiced many of these concerns. Why had Elizabeth Daniels not raised the alarm earlier, instead of waiting until the following day to instigate a search for her missing stepson? She also seemed to undergo a complete change of manner and temperament. It was remarked that, before John's death, she was:

very gay, singing and merry, and has since affected to sing but it is
observed by the neighbourhood that she pined away. Her lips wale, and
in this time in an infirm way.

Of course, it could equally be argued that the profound
change in her personality might have easily been caused by
grief and not guilt. Coupled with the rumour that John had
nominated his stepmother as 'Lord's next tenant' over his
landholdings, which he was due to inherit on his fourteenth
birthday, Elizabeth Daniel seemed to have both motive and
opportunity to have murdered her stepson.

Rumours and speculation, however, do not constitute
proof and no charges were ever brought against John's
stepmother, nor against anyone else.

Although the chilling appearance of the ethereal being
in St Mary's Church may have finally revealed the truth
regarding the death of John Daniel, it failed to see anyone
brought to justice for the boy's murder. The story, it
seemed, was at an end. Or was it?

Even several weeks after the sensational events of 22nd June,
allegations and speculation still simmered under the surface
in Beaminster. However, life was beginning to return to
normal in the small town. The women tended to their
children and chores, and the menfolk toiled in the fields
under the hot summer sun, then quenched their thirst in
the town's many inns. Most of the townspeople still went to
church on Sunday, with the more devout parishioners also
attending the midweek service. It was at one such service,
on Wednesday 7th August, that events would once again
take an unexpected turn.

If the bizarre experience suffered by the schoolboys on 22nd June might have been dismissed as a prank or youthful exuberance, then the events of 7th August were felt by a healthy congregation of 'devout parishioners' of differing ages, including a fourteen -year-old girl known to be 'of very good repute for her veracity' (according to the contemporary account).

The girl, a servant, was kneeling at prayer in the gallery of St Mary's Church, the area of the church which also doubled as a schoolroom. Her employer was knelt in the row in front. She was momentarily distracted by some movement below, as the door adjacent to the stairway leading up to the gallery opened. The door opening appears to have made no sound, since the young girl's master did not turn around. Framed in the open doorway, silhouetted by the evening light from the churchyard, was a gaunt, pale woman who seemed to be looking up towards to the gallery, as if searching for someone. The girl assumed that the woman in the doorway was looking for her master. He had a young daughter at home who had been taken ill. Perhaps the woman had been sent to the church to convey an urgent message to him regarding his daughter's condition. Assuming this to be the case, the servant girl tapped her master on the shoulder and informed him that a woman wished to speak to him. Fearing the worst, the man rushed down the stairs only for the door to slam loudly in front of him. A split-second later, he opened the door, fully expecting to see the woman outside. However, there was no one in sight. He searched:

behind the buttresses of the church wall and corners and all about but could see nobody, which increased his surprise for it was impossible for any human creature to get out of the churchyard in so short a time.

The noise of the church door slamming was heard by the entire congregation including the minister. All were knelt in silent prayer at that moment, and all turned around with a start. Everyone present seemed baffled, the night was still, and a gust of wind could not have caused the door to slam shut. Neither was anyone stood close enough to have shut the door. The servant girl was asked to describe the woman she had witnessed in the doorway, and her description was recorded. According to the girl, the woman at the church door appeared thin and gaunt with a pale countenance, yet 'rosier with the pox'. She described the woman's dress as a 'sad' or dark-coloured gown (possibly a mourning outfit), with a straw hat and a flowered handkerchief. Those present agreed that the girl's description seemed to match that of John Daniel's real mother, Hannah, who had passed away shortly after John's birth in 1714. The contemporary account from the time also added another rather intriguing detail, 'And it is to be observed, that the girl who saw her could not possibly describe her, being born about the same time of her death.'

It is certainly possible that Hannah Daniel had succumbed to the dreaded 'pox'. Smallpox was widespread and virulent during the eighteenth-century. Dorset was particularly susceptible, due to its proximity to several seaports. Indeed, the disease, with a mortality rate of 30%, killed more than 400,000 Europeans almost every year of that century. In Dorset, most of the population became infected with the virus. Many towns and villages in the county operated 'Pest Houses' to quarantine the infected and, such was the extent of the problem, that a Dorset farmer named Benjamin Jesty from Yetminster, experimented with a cowpox vaccine many years before Edward Jenner.

Had the ghost of John Daniel's mother returned to grieve over her son and the failure to bring his killer to justice? Many townsfolk certainly believed so. Yet, despite these two widely witnessed events, no killer was brought to justice for the apparent murder of John Daniel. Nevertheless, it seems that the ghost of John Daniel would not rest.

Over the following two centuries there were more scattered sightings of John Daniel's ghost in the churchyard at St Mary's. Reports of a vision, noting the sudden appearance of a 'sad child' or a 'tearful child' have occurred with enough frequency to warrant an entry in Britain's Paranormal Database (an online archive in which unexplained sightings and experiences are recorded). However, it would not be until 270 years later that events took a dramatic turn.

In August 1998, Peter Beer, a Beaminster dairy farmer, was making an early morning visit to check on his herd of cows on Knowle Farm. The cows were about to calve, hence the early start. It was 4.45am and sunrise was still an hour away. The twilight did not provide enough illumination to see unaided and he carried a torch with him. As he approached, something unexpected seemed to loom in the shadowy, half-light ahead. Mr Beer would later describe the unfolding events for the *Bridport Times*:

One of the cows had calved and as I switched on my powerful torch to see where she was, I saw two figures standing by the cow, just as if they were watching it calve. I picked it out to be a woman, because she was wearing a sort of long white gown, and the boy had a dark outfit.

I was only standing about ten paces away. The woman turned around to look at me. She had pink eyes. The cow got up and walked out of their way. Then the two of them walked towards the graveyard and I heard the gates open and shut – that really spooked me.

Mr Beer froze momentarily, before running back to his farmhouse to tell his wife about the 'spectral figures' he had seen. His frightened appearance shocked his wife, who told the *Bridport Times* that she had never seen him so petrified.

Could the unearthly manifestation have been the forlorn Hannah Daniel and her son John? There are three reasons that seem to add credence to Mr Beer's chilling experience. Firstly, the field in which the strange event took place adjoins the private Daniel family graveyard. When daylight dawned, Peter Beer returned to the field and visited the graveyard, 'For my own peace of mind, I had to go back and find out if there was a grave with a woman and child in it.' Among the headstones he found one overgrown and worn grave which sent chills down his spine – that of a man, woman, and child. Could it have been the final resting place of Isaac Daniel, Hannah and John?

Secondly, just days before this incident, Mr Beer had been contacted by a descendant of the Daniel family who wished to visit the family cemetery and had even contacted Beaminster Town Council in the hope of restoring the overgrown and tumbledown graveyard. Had the spirits of his predecessors been somehow awakened?

Thirdly, for those who believe in numerology (the power of numbers) perhaps the dates are significant. The appearance of the ghostly figures seems to coincide with the anniversary of John Daniel's 14th birthday. The number 14 is of huge significance in religions throughout the world. John died (or was murdered) shortly before his 14th birthday, the age of the angel, the age at which the wronged person can pass on messages of misdeeds done in their past, or to indicate the immense pressure a person may have to endure in life and death. In Chinese spiritualism, 14 is interpreted as 'guaranteed death'. In the Bible it represents deliverance from salvation, God delivered the firstborn of Israel from death on the 14th day of the month. In fact, such is its significance, that the number appears on no less than 65 further occasions in the Bible. Eerily, the vision at Knowle Farm appeared to Mr Beer exactly 284 years after the anniversary of John's birth – 2+8+4 = 14, or 270 years after John's death – 2x7+0 = 14. Hannah passed away in 1714, and John in 1728; 14 years later.

For those who require a slightly more historical and tangible explanation, the current owner of the graveyard believes there is no firm evidence that John Daniel is buried there. Although it is also believed that a relation of the murdered schoolboy, Sarah Anne Daniel, may also haunt the graveyard.

There is a record of horses rearing in fear in the face of an angry apparition as they approached the site during a funeral in 1773.

Even in more recent years, St Mary's Church has witnessed another strange manifestation. During the summer of 2006, while some restoration work was being undertaken at the church, a workman heard a sudden knock on the south door of the building. As he walked towards the door to open it, he noticed a person's shadow moving in the light under the door. According to *The Book of Beaminster*, curated by Beaminster Museum:

He looked outside but nobody was there. Then a dark figure, whose presence could not be logically explained was seen in the church. The following morning the trail of a child's footprints were discovered in sand that had been laid for paving, and the word "PEACE" written in the sand, yet nothing had been noticed the previous evening. Two days later the workman heard a howling gale coming under the west door but when he looked outside it was flat calm.

However, the ghostly and unexplained experiences witnessed during the past three centuries in Beaminster do not help us understand two fundamental questions: Was John Daniel murdered and, if he was, then who was his killer?

Firstly, the prime suspect in his death was undoubtedly his stepmother, Elizabeth. She appears to have possessed both motive (John was due to inherit the right of 'Lord's next tenant' on his fourteenth birthday), and the means – she would undoubtedly have had ample opportunity. It was also noted that she failed to organise any search for her stepson until the following day. Yet, there are several fatal objections to this argument. Would a woman really possess the strength to strangle a fourteen-year-old boy, without leaving any signs of a struggle, and then haul his body to a remote spot 220 yards from their home? Add to this the very singular fact that no attempt was made to hide the body, and that no one overheard screaming or a commotion. Elizabeth Daniel's explanation that John regularly suffered from fits seems to have been accepted without hesitation. This strongly suggests that others may have witnessed him suffering from a fit or seizure in the weeks leading to his death; and therefore, not challenged her explanation.

Secondly, if Elizabeth Daniel really had strangled her own stepson, would she have allowed two neighbours to help her dress and prepare his body for interment, and failed to adequately cover up the markings around the victim's throat?

Elizabeth Daniel was criticised for failing to organise a search until the following day. However, perhaps John regularly stayed out all night, looking after the calving cows for example. We simply do not know.

Yet, if Elizabeth Daniel did not strangle her stepson, then how, or by whom, was he murdered? Who would possibly want to kill a schoolboy? One of his fellow pupils, conceivably? This seems unlikely, firstly John was one of the oldest and biggest of the pupils at Beaminster School, and by all accounts a popular child. Secondly, there is no evidence to support this theory. Perhaps a violent assault or robbery, then? Again, there is little in the way of contemporary evidence to support this. It is unlikely that a schoolboy would be in possession of a large amount of money. There were no other marks of violence on John's body, no sign of a robbery, and no mention of other similar attacks or undesirable strangers passing through the area. Normally, in such unexplained deaths, passing itinerant travellers or labourers would be among the first to be blamed for any crimes committed in the area.

This seems to leave two other alternatives.

If Elizabeth Daniel did, in fact, murder her stepson perhaps it was by another method altogether? One other favoured technique among female killers does immediately spring to mind – poison. Arsenic, for example was regularly used as a rat poison, and also as a method of murder in the eighteenth-century. Arsenic could be easily disguised in food or drink and, although exposure to the poison frequently also left markings and inflammation on the skin, there was no known test to detect arsenic poisoning until 1836. Another readily available toxin also springs to mind. The poisonous water hemlock plant grew (and still grows) abundantly in Dorset, particularly around damp areas such as ditches and streams. In fact, there have been cases of pet dogs dying from the ingestion of hemlock in Dorset as recently as 2020. Among the many symptoms associated with hemlock poisoning is the appearance of a red rash, streaking, or blistering on the skin, and the inability of the victim to cry out.

Perhaps either of these methods of poisoning, or even a herbal remedy, might just as easily explain the location and situation of John's body by the stream, as well as account for his death. However, with no scientific evidence it is now impossible to prove this theory.

Finally, we should not overlook the possibility that a great injustice has been done to Elizabeth Daniel. Perhaps John really did suffer from regular fits or seizures, such as epilepsy? The 'falling sickness' as it was then known, did not benefit from more modern diagnosis or treatment for a least a century after John's sad demise. Remember, no one challenged Elizabeth Daniel's claim that John had suffered from fits, not even his younger half-brother. John had damaged his hand in the days prior to his death. Conceivably he may have fallen during a fit. A sudden seizure or fit might also explain the strange location and 'unnatural position' in which his body was discovered. Certain types of seizures are also known to leave tell-tale bruising and skin trauma on the victim's body.

The second innocent explanation for John Daniel's death is the more commonplace one in eighteenth-century England. Perhaps he succumbed to smallpox, like so many others did each year. It is certainly possible that his real mother may have also died from the disease. Again, this would explain the presence of markings on John's skin and the unusual location of the body. He may have simply staggered there in a weakened state. Rather eerily, inflamed and reddened eyes are another symptom of an untreated smallpox infection – remarkably similar to the 'bright pink eyes' witnessed by Peter Beer during his ghostly encounter in 1998.

Whether Elizabeth Daniel was guilty of her stepson's murder or not, she appears to have remained in Beaminster among the Daniel family, despite strong local suspicions. She married a local man, Henry Gould, a year or so later. Her son, Isaac junior, became a farmer and tanner. He married Mary Clark and lived out the remainder of his life in the town, apparently untroubled by further visions of his half-brother.

Whilst the true cause of John Daniel's death will probably never be known, one thing is certain. A traumatic, unexpected and unnatural death seems to have caused the haunted and restless spirit of a tearful and forlorn schoolboy to haunt the shadows of St Mary's Church for almost three centuries.

THE PORTLAND PRISON MUTINY

We waited for the sun
To break its cloudy prison.

Thomas Hardy, *In the Garden*, 1915

In 1846, with concern growing over the possibility of a
French invasion, it was decided to construct breakwaters
and a series of harbour defences on the Isle of Portland
in Dorset. In order to provide the colossal amount of
labour needed for this ambitious project, the government
announced that a public works prison would be built in
an area of Portland known as Verne Hill. The massive
structure, complete with towering walls, would be erected
on common land, close to the village of Grove, on the east
of the island, and was designed to house 800 men in cells
seven feet in length, four feet wide, and seven feet high.
Most of the convicts incarcerated there would be utilised in
hewing stone from the nearby Admiralty Quarries. Others
would be put to work constructing the various buildings
and facilities. 1,300 paid workers were also employed to
work alongside the prisoners, a situation fraught with
problems, which would later materialise.

On arrival at Portland Prison, each convict was given a period of solitary confinement, before undertaking their back-breaking sentence, labouring in the construction of the breakwater. Once their mandatory endeavours had been completed, they would be transported to the Australian colonies. If a man performed his tasks satisfactorily, and without causing trouble, he would be granted a 'Ticket of Leave', entitling him to certain freedoms once in Australia, such as the ability to seek certain types of employment, and the chance to qualify for a return passage to England (after a designated period of time).

The number of prisoners housed at Portland soon grew from 800 to 1,500. The convict labour was expected to produce 10,000 tons of stone per week for use on the breakwater. Huge blocks of stone were squared, heaved into wagons, and transported via the Admiralty Incline Railway down to the harbour.

Conditions were harsh. In the warmer weather the hot sun beat down unmercifully on the prisoners. Many men died during the construction and prison warders were frequently assaulted. Three prison guards were also murdered, resulting in the executions of the men responsible.

It would not be long before the newly established prison and quarrying brought curious, genteel Victorian tourists to the area. Postcards showing scenes of the convicts toiling were printed. In the 1912 preface to his novel, *The Well-Beloved*, Thomas Hardy even referred to the strange attraction created by the prison - 'The retreat, at their country's expense.' Attracted by a combination of grotesque and curious fascination, sightseers also flocked to a number of cafes and tearooms that were quickly established by residents in the upper rooms of their homes along Grove Road.

Unsurprisingly, the prison at Portland has witnessed many escape attempts during its lifetime. These were mostly by desperate individuals, or small groups, unhappy with the conditions or hoping to avoid transportation to the colonies in a disease-ridden prison ship. Convicts felt a bitter sense of injustice, with no recourse but to attempt escape. Victorian society's view of the criminal classes, and especially the hardened criminal, are perfectly encapsulated in this opinion expressed by an aggrieved letter writer to *The Times*, shortly before dramatic events that were to take place in 1858:

There are always from 1,400 to 1,600 convicts at Portland, mostly working in gangs, in close proximity to groups of free labourers. On the steep headlands around, stalk the tall figures of the warders. They carry their rifles ready and seem all eyes and ears as they scan the ground beneath them like eager sportsmen looking for a shot. The prisoners look like pugilists, ready for a fight, with their slow, lazy style of working, or rather moving, which contrasts with the busy energy and speed of the free workmen near at hand. These are men of infamy, poachers, burglars, murderers, the most inveterate of all ruffians, who have known every form of punishment known to the law – short of hanging. These slothful labourers are alike in their vicious and forbidding aspect – their low, narrow retreating foreheads, keen, restless eyes, and vindictive animal features.

During the stifling summer heat of 1858 dissatisfaction grew among the toiling convicts, resulting in a number of unsuccessful attempted escapes. This only served to fuel the sense of resentment felt by the inmates, and to sharpen the wits of their guards.

Each convict was paid between twelve and fifteen shillings per week for their labours, which they used to purchase tobacco, and probably to bribe the free workmen in the quarries to furnish them with supplies. During late August and early September of 1858, a rumour began to circulate that the Portland convicts were planning to strike for better wages. Worried government officials also believed that the intended strike might be a cover for an attempted breakout. The tense atmosphere in the jail was palpable. Had agitators among the prison population paid, bribed, or intimidated the free labourers employed in the quarries to supply weapons or somehow distract the guards?

The convicts were divided into clearly defined groups. Any prisoner who had previously attempted escape was dressed in a grey and yellow prison uniform, those who had made

threats of violence towards the warders wore grey and
black. Armed guards were placed along the raised divisions
between the east, west, and central parts of the government
quarry, along which the raised tramways conveyed the
stone down to the breakwater.

Fearing a conspiracy, 200 civil guards and warders were
strategically placed at several vantage points along the 500-
yard route from the prison gates down to the curved stone
wall surrounding the quarry. In addition, half a mile from
the jail, 150 extra soldiers from the Wexford Militia were
placed in barracks on the Verne Hill fortification. It was
also rumoured that the government had secretly inserted a
spy, either among the free workmen employed in quarrying,
or even among the prison population. Next, an official
observer was placed in quarters at Portland, with special
instructions to highlight any troublemakers, and to report
on any disruptive behaviour among the prisoners. Whenr
being collected from Weymouth by his appointed driver, he
was warned to ensure that he had remembered to pack his
revolver - just in case.

At 7.15am on Monday 19th September 1858 the prison
gates clanked open, and a steady stream of convict work
parties emerged into the morning sunshine. Special
instructions had been given for each work detail to be
guarded by at least two armed warders. Body searches
were conducted to ensure the men were not concealing
any tobacco or weapons about their person. The work
teams then steadily poured through the gates for twenty
minutes until approximately 1,000 men could be viewed
snaking their way along the roadway towards the quarry.
For practical reasons, the men selected for the physically

demanding work were the largest and strongest at the institution. Heavy prison chains had also been removed, to allow the men to work more freely. The government observer, from his secure vantage point, noted that the men seemed to be 'the most formidable ruffians I have ever seen.'

For a few minutes all seemed as normal. The morning sunshine was already warm as the men put on their prison jackets and caps and readied themselves for the backbreaking toil of the day. The guards visibly relaxed, perhaps hoping that rumours of a planned mass escape had been exaggerated. However, a careful onlooker might have observed the tense, sullen demeanour on the faces of the ringleaders and the furtive glances between the various work parties. The signal to commence work was given but was initially ignored. It seemed as if the convicts were awaiting a signal which had not yet arrived. Again, the order to begin digging and hewing was given and once more it was ignored. The guards gripped their rifles a little tighter, anticipating the worst.

Then, in a moment of relief, tensions seemed to subside as the convicts picked up their assorted pickaxes and shovels and began to begrudgingly begin the day's work. During the summer months, nine hours of work was expected every day, and any delay might compromise the government's plans to fortify the island against French incursion. The guards relaxed a little as the work parties concentrated once again on the task in hand digging, then squaring large lumps of stone, before heaving them onto wagons waiting on the tramway.

It is not known if the ringleaders among the convicts had noticed the warders visibly relaxing, or whether a signal had been pre-arranged for the optimum moment, but after an hour of toil a convict in the most central work party suddenly yelled out 'NOW!' In a flash, thirty or forty convicts broke formation and rushed towards the raised tramway, jumping on the open wagons. As they ran forward, the ringleaders screamed out to their comrades, urging them to join the revolt. Another large throng of prisoners began to surge forward.

The outnumbered guards seemed to be taken by surprise, at least initially, and did not react. No reinforcements appeared to assist the warders, and the gathering mob, realising this, pushed forward tentatively, slowly growing in numbers. Then, a seemingly well-rehearsed signal was passed among the warders, a shout was given, and a picket of twelve well-armed men from the Wexford Militia sprang from their hiding place and fearlessly charged down the sloping side of the quarry. The soldiers hurried along the line of the tramway in close order, with their gleaming bayonets already fixed to their Enfield rifles. In a matter of moments, they confronted the first band of conspirators, who looked on in utter astonishment and dismay at the speed and surprise of the attack. The convicts halted in their tracks, hesitated for a moment, before dropping their tools and fleeing away from the soldiers.

As they turned to run, a bugle was sounded from somewhere above and yet more soldiers sprang out from pre-arranged places of concealment and aimed their rifles at the larger group of convicts. In a moment, every potential hiding place had been sealed off, and the convicts were split from each other into weaker, more manageable groups. In the meantime, the remainder of the Wexfords, under the direction of Captain Pigott, took up elevated positions along the quarry, their rifles trained on the main body of convicts below them. With every salient point of escape covered, the initial group of forty troublemakers were herded at bayonet point into a corrugated iron shed. Once inside, the warders shackled the men together while a dozen soldiers covered them, rifles and bayonets at the ready.

Now safely chained, the men were marched back inside the prison and into solitary confinement cells. Meanwhile, the remaining throng of convicts resigned themselves to defeat and, cursing and muttering, picked up their picks and shovels and returned to their designated workplaces.

As the sun relentlessly beat down on the convicts, tempers once again reached boiling point. On three more occasions during the day a small group of convicts made a desperate rush from the sides of the quarry towards the raised tramway in the centre, but each time they were easily captured, either by the Wexford soldiers, or the armed warders (who had now been issued with swords). Yet more men were dragged into solitary confinement. As night fell, and the 'Lights out!' signal sounded around the prison, the sickening sound of the lash from the 'cat-o-nine tails on bare flesh echoed around the compound.

The following morning, Tuesday, the convicts were once again marched outside to commence work, having been woken at 5am. They appeared sullen and beaten, as they picked up their tools to begin the day's toil. Suddenly another shout of 'NOW!' echoed out around the base of the quarry and a group of twenty men rushed from the western end towards the centre. However, just as on the previous day, a strategically placed unit of Wexford Troops, commanded by Captain Allcock, appeared from the raised road between the quarries and quickly subdued the prisoners.

This continued spasmodically throughout the remainder of the day. Each time the insurgents were easily halted, then herded away to be chained and punished. By the end of the day, the bulk of the convicts seemed to have admitted defeat. Some even voluntarily walked inside the corrugated iron shed to be shackled.

The following day, Wednesday, it was thought sufficiently safe to allow the Government observer access to the quarry and prison to ascertain and report on developments.

Those convicts who were labelled 'agitators' by the authorities were dealt with harshly, which meant the lash of the 'cat' and an extended period of solitary confinement, before being transferred to Millbank Prison in London and, directly from there, transportation to Australia.

Those who did not initiate, but merely took part, in the attempted breakout, seem to have been treated remarkably lightly, although the presence of the Wexford Militia appears to have been a calming influence. Frighteningly, some of the prison warders had fully intended to inflict their own brand of instant and harsh justice on the convicts. At one stage during the rioting a junior officer in the Wexfords bravely stood between the throng of convicts and the warders to prevent any shots being fired.

The ringleaders among the prisoners were questioned regarding the planning and reasoning behind the escape attempt, by Captain Gambier, Director of the warders, and Captain Clay, Governor of the prison.

The official version of the convicts' plan, as later published in the press, was:

To rush from the outlying parts of the quarries, to concentrate in the centre and arm themselves with hammers and picks, then overpower and murder the guards, burn the prison, plunder the villages, and make their escape to the mainland before assistance could arrive.

However, this scarcely seems a likely admission for the prisoners to have made, and was no doubt forced, exaggerated, or falsified. However, it did achieve the desired effect of horrifying the public and causing hysteria among the newspaper editors, who rushed to condemn the scenes at Portland. One reporter followed the line of men being transferred to Millbank Prison, remarking that:

I watched as the chained men were marched out. I accompanied them a considerable distance along the road, it was only then I fully appreciated the extent of the danger which had been averted, or understood what would have happened had they obtained mastery. I can only compare them to a gang of demons baffled in a conspiracy against mankind, steeped in crime, and openly displaying their atrocity, villainy, and rage at the failure of their plot.

He went further, explaining to his readership just how well treated the inmates at Portland had been, and in what 'luxury' they were housed:

Everything in the prison is as clean and orderly as a gentleman's house. The prison is wide and lofty, well lighted and ventilated, yet kept comfortably warm. The prisoners' dinners are carefully got ready, weighed out, and served smoking hot in bright clean tins. In addition to their dinners the men receive a treacle pudding on Thursdays, baked mutton on Fridays, and baked beef instead of boiled beef on Sundays and Mondays! It seems almost a farce to call their labour 'hard labour'. It seems little more than excuse for keeping them out-of-doors for a certain time. Even those who took part in the riots received only the light sentence of two-or-three dozen lashes!

Despite the gripes of the establishment, it appears that many of the convicts incarcerated at Portland felt that they had genuine grievances over their sentencing. The terms of the *Penal Servitude Act 1853*, and several amendments to the Act that followed four years later, stirred up a great deal of resentment and confusion among those affected. An unlucky prisoner was often sentenced to hard labour followed by transportation, when, in fact, the Act originally stipulated either one punishment or the other.

Many of the convicts imprisoned at Portland had been sentenced under the terms of the 1853 Act. However, those who had been convicted more recently, under the 1857 amendments to the Act, were entitled to remission for good behaviour. This seemed grossly unjust to those men sentenced earlier. However, as Captain Clay, the Governor at Portland, pointed out to the prisoners, this amendment – while seeming to be entirely fair in theory – played out much differently in practice. Following the passing of the *1857 Penal Servitude Amendment Act*, judges merely passed a five-year sentence (fully expecting a year's remission to be granted), instead of the old four-year sentences which had previously been handed out during the era of the 1853 Act.

In addition, the attempted escape from Portland was used by the government to justify its recent controversial changes to the Act, which also included the ability to extend sentences for prisoner misconduct and to substitute hard labour for transportation, and vice versa. In fact, any hope that the riot at Portland might bring public attention to the harsh conditions endured by convicts, seems to have had the opposite effect. In 1861, the *Offences Against the Person Act* further widened the authorities' ability to sentence prisoners to terms of penal servitude. As well as including the traditional crimes of murder, rape, and wounding with intent, the remit to prescribe a sentence of hard labour now included more minor offences such as petty theft and vagrancy. Even so-called 'victimless behaviour deemed harmful to society' was included, such as Oscar Wilde's infamous imprisonment with hard labour in 1895.

Those convicts at Portland Jail involved in the back breaking effort to construct the breakwater were finally relieved of the task when the mammoth project was eventually completed in 1872. The injustice and cruelty of the transportation system had been ended four years earlier; however, prisoners would have a much longer wait until the joint prison punishments of hard labour and the lash were finally removed with the passing of the *Criminal Justice Act* in 1948, a full ninety years after the attempted breakout from Portland Prison.

British Justice in the nineteenth century, it seems, leapt more willingly towards harsher punishment, than it crawled reluctantly towards reform and understanding.

TRAGEDY IN SILVER LANE

I think that whenever children be born that are not wanted they should be killed directly, before their souls come to 'em, and not allowed to grow big and walk about!

Thomas Hardy, *Jude the Obscure*, 1895

On Sunday 19ᵗʰ May 1889 a dark and disturbing incident cast a shadow over the peaceful village of Rockbeare in Devonshire. Now in the administrative region of East Devon, the community does not derive its name from the former quarry, but simply means 'the rooks in the grove'. Traditionally an ominous presence, perhaps the encircling rooks foreshadowed the events of that Sunday in 1889?

The weather had been fine and warm and Frederick Hallett, a 12-year-old schoolboy was enjoying his day off from school. During that Sunday afternoon he happened to be wandering in the fields between Silver Lane and Rockbeare Manor. Silver Lane was a quiet, narrow lane running south from the village towards the small settlement of Little Silver. To the west lay Woodhouse Farm and to the east, across the fields in which Frederick sauntered, sat Limes Farms and the imposing Georgian estate of

Rockbeare Manor. The young boy stopped for a while by the large pond next to the stream and idly prodded the bank with a stick and tossed a handful of stones into the muddy water.

Something half floating in the murky waters of the pond caught his eye. He fished the item out with a stick, pulling it up onto the bank. It appeared to be a cloth bag or parcel, tightly wrapped with cord. Unwrapping the sodden package, Frederick Hallett cautiously untied the bag, then recoiled with horror as the decomposed body of a small child slowly revealed itself to him. The boy, momentarily paralysed with shock, quickly gathered his wits, before running off in the direction of Rockbeare to fetch assistance. Several villagers returned with Frederick, to the spot where he had first discovered the child's body. On realising that Frederick was not exaggerating or mistaken, an urgent message was sent to police Constable Heywood who was stationed in the village of Aylesbeare, a couple of miles to the south. The constable arrived at the scene an hour or so later and examined the bag. He noticed that the package had been weighed down with two large stones. After sending an urgent telegram to Superintendent Herbert De Schmid in Exeter, and Dr James Somers, the Devon surgeon, the baby's body was removed to the Crown and Sceptre Inn in Rockbeare, ready to be examined the following morning.

After the shock of these distressing circumstances, PC Heywood returned to Aylesbeare, only to discover that a mysterious and anonymous letter had been posted through the letter box of his cottage. He carefully opened the folded sheet on which the following words were written:

Mrs Emma Hallett, the wife of William Hallett the labourer, who lives in Silver Lane, Rockbeare, appears to have had a child. Is it right for a married woman to conceal a birth?

The handwritten note was unsigned but appeared to PC Heywood to be in a woman's hand. The lady named in the letter lived just a few hundred yards from the pond in which the grim discovery had been made. Coincidentally, Frederick Hallett, the boy who had first found the body, was a nephew of William and Emma Hallett.

Dr Somers examined the body on Monday morning and immediately instructed PC Heywood that an official inquest would be required, which was hastily arranged for the following day. Mr Charles Cox, the deputy coroner for the district was summoned, as was Superintendent De Schmid, William and Emma Hallett, and several witnesses from the village.

When the inquest opened on Tuesday 21st May 1889, there were several matters to be considered. Even assuming that a child had been stillborn, a sadly common occurrence in Victorian England, it was still considered an offence under the *Offences Against the Person Act* of 1861 for:

Any woman who shall be delivered of a child, and every person who shall, by any secret disposal of the dead body of the said child, whether such child died before, at, or after its birth, endeavour to conceal the birth thereof, shall be guilty of a misdemeanour, and being convicted thereof, shall be liable at the discretion of the Court, to be imprisoned for any term not exceeding two years, with or without Hard Labour.

If, however, it was discovered that the child was 'still alive when disposed of or, if the child had been deliberately killed in order to necessitate such a course of action', the charge of wilful murder could be imposed.

Sadly, unwanted pregnancies were a depressing part of everyday life in Victorian England. Whatever the reason, whether it be social stigma, poor health, the fear of giving birth out of wedlock, or poverty, expectant mothers would frequently hide their pregnancy in the hope that the child could be disposed of secretly. An even more sinister method of removing unwanted children reared its head in both Devon and Dorset in the late Victorian era, which we will return to later.

Dr James Somers spoke first at the inquest to report on the results of his post-mortem examination. His findings must have been as traumatic for those present in the cramped conditions at the Crown and Sceptre, as they are today:

*I examined the body upon the instructions of the Coroner. It was
partly wrapped in an old bag, and had a piece of the skirt of a dress
tied tightly around the chest. When this was removed, the body was
in such a decomposed state that the skin came away with the cloth. I
found the body to be that of a fully-developed female child, twenty-
one inches in length, and the lungs, when subjected to the usual test,
showed that the child had breathed. The umbilical chord had been tied
with a piece of stay lace.*

*From the appearance of the body I am of the opinion that the child
had been dead about ten days to a fortnight, but it may have been a
longer or shorter time, and was probably suffocated by the piece of
skirt which had been tied in a tight manner around the chest.*

And is it possible drowning caused the death of the child? asked the
Coroner.

*Death might possibly have been caused by drowning, but I do not think
that was the case.*

The coroner next spoke to Mrs Emma Hallett, brandishing
as he did so, the anonymous handwritten note written to
PC Heywood:

*Mrs Hallett, for the purposes of this inquest, please identify yourself
to those present.*

*Sir, I am Emma Hallett, the wife of William Hallett, I am between
forty-seven and forty-eight years of age and the mother of four living
children.*

*And have you recently been confined with child or given birth, as
referred to in this letter?*

*No, sir. I have not. My youngest being fifteen years of age. The last
occasion on which I was confined was eleven or twelve years ago, and
the child was stillborn.*

And is there any truth in this letter claiming you have recently been with child?

No sir, I deny everything in that letter. It is not true.

The next witness to be summoned made her way nervously to the front of the room. Sarah Mortimore was both Emma Hallett's next-door neighbour and sister-in-law and no doubt felt extremely awkward at the direct line of questioning from the coroner. Charles Cox had been a solicitor for many years before being appointed coroner, and he would later serve the Liberal Party with distinction.

Mrs Mortimore, did you write the anonymous letter sent to the police?

No, sir. And any jury can think what they like.

Then can you say who did write this note?

I cannot, no.

Please tell this inquest when you last saw Mrs Hallett.

Sir, I have seen her many times in the past two or three months and I did notice changes in her appearance.

And what did you conclude from these changes?

Well, I supposed she had again become a mother.

And did you see her on the 3rd May?

Yes, sir. I saw her. I thought she was carrying a roll of carpet. But I only saw her from some way off.

And do you have anything further to add?

Yes, sir. Mrs Hallett kept her door closed for three or four days around that time. She didn't usually do that. I remarked to my husband that it seemed very quiet next door. I also believe she went away around that time, to stay at a farm in North Devon I believe.

And did you ask Mrs Hallett why it was that she had kept her door closed and had been so quiet? asked Mr Cox.

No sir. Although we live in adjoining houses we are not on speaking terms, on account of my husband, her brother, having fallen out with her. But that is not all, sir. My husband also noticed an unusual smell on Tuesday night, the 14th May, as he was coming home. It was a little after nine o'clock.

And what caused this unusual smell, Mrs Mortimore?

We could not come to any conclusion about it, sir, and my husband could not suggest the cause of it; but he did consider that the smell came from the Hallett's house.

Could not the smell have come from somewhere else, Mrs Mortimore?

The smell did not come from the fields where Mr Symons carries on his manure factory.

Mrs Mortimore, does not a manure factory seem like a more likely cause of an unusual smell? Mr Cox asked, with a look of some incredulity.

Well, my husband said he'd never noticed any offensive smell from the fields before. And, when he called my attention to the smell, I went outside and noticed that it was very peculiar. It was very strong out in the road as the wind blew across from the chimney.

And you assumed the smell came the chimney, Mrs Mortimore?

Yes, sir. I thought it came from the chimney, and it was the smell of something burning, but I could not come to a conclusion over what caused it, sir.

And did no one else notice this unusual smell of burning, Mrs Mortimore?

No, I did not mention it to anyone else.

But you remember it clearly, nevertheless?

Yes, sir. It is strongly in my mind because the very next day was the first time I noticed Mrs Hallett was slighter in her appearance.

Thank you, Mrs Mortimore.

Next to be called was Mrs Ruth Drew who garnered the wrath of both the coroner and Superintendent De Schmid by completely reversing the statement she had given to the police just twenty-four hours earlier:

I have seen Mrs Hallett many times since the end of April, she stated, *and I have not noticed any change in her appearance before or since.*

At this point Superintendent De Schmid became so irritated, he interrupted the proceedings to challenge Mrs Drew directly:

Mrs Drew, this evidence is the exact opposite to your previous statement. Did you not comment to another neighbour (Mrs Marks) *on Good Friday about the change in Mrs Hallett's appearance and said that, I quote, 'It was a bad job?*

I don't remember that, I might have used those words. I am only reminded of it as other people say I said that.

Mr Cox interjected with some impatience, *Do you wish to adhere to that statement or this one?*

I only know it was Good Friday because other folk told Mrs Hallett about it. I never said anything to her on the subject; and I do not remember using the words referred to.

The coroner, plainly annoyed, dismissed Mrs Drew, cautioning her as she stepped down,

I consider your evidence most unsatisfactory, Mrs Drew.

Mrs Maria Marks, the wife of the church sexton, testified to knowing Emma Hallett for twenty-seven years:

I passed her near Broadclyst Station on the 3ʳᵈ of May. I noticed a difference in her appearance. I had not seen her for sometime before that, perhaps four months. I noticed there was a great change in her. She was walking as if tired out and hardly able to get along. I had heard reports about her from others, which led me to form my opinion.

And what did else did you notice, Mrs Marks? asked the coroner.

Well, sir, she was carrying a bag or something, it was not very large or small.

Was this bag or parcel she was carrying the reason she seemed to be struggling to walk, or because she appeared "tired out", as you mentioned earlier?

I do not think so, sir, replied the sexton's wife.

But it might be possible for a woman carrying a load to appear different than she would without one?

I suppose so, answered Mrs Marks.

Maria Marks was then dismissed and Dr James Somers was recalled to present some further medical evidence. This time it was Superintendent De Schmid who questioned him:

Dr Somers, I believe you were asked to call professionally on Mrs Mortimore on Saturday May 25th?

Indeed. On leaving the house, Mr Hallett, the neighbour, requested that I look in upon his wife. He said that rumours spreading in the village about Mrs Hallett were untrue; but that the sergeant of police had requested that I should examine her, with her consent.

And did Mrs Hallett allow such an examination, doctor?

She offered not the least objection.

And what did you observe, doctor?

Mrs Hallett was weak but otherwise well. I found no evidence that she had recently been delivered of a child, but it is very difficult to state positively after between ten and fourteen days from the time of confinement. But in my opinion, she had not.

Thank you, Doctor Somers.

With the inquest proceedings then nearing their conclusion, the coroner summed up the evidence for the benefit of the jury:

Members of the jury, according to the opinion of the doctor, the child was born between the 7th and 11th of May, and that it was born alive being the most important point. Upon the circumstances attending the discovery of the child's body and the doctor's examination, the case appears to be an extremely serious one.

The body being found under such conditions, it might naturally be presumed to have got where it was in a very improper way. Furthermore, the condition in which the child was found, and the opinion of the doctor that the child was clearly born alive and met its death by means of suffocation, would raise in ordinary minds the presumption that the child was wilfully murdered. Therefore, it is for you, the jury, to consider by whom the murder was committed.

In considering the question it was of the utmost importance to ascertain, if possible, who was the mother of the child, because the mother was its natural guardian and protector; and it was almost impossible to suppose that the child had been placed where it was, and in such a condition, without some kind of knowledge on her part, In the absence of her coming forward and acknowledging that she was indeed the mother, and explaining so far as she could how the child got where it was, there is naturally a very great suspicion against her being a party in its death.

The question, therefore, of the utmost importance was, if possible, to ascertain who was in fact the mother of the child. With regard to that point, there have been rumours circulated by anonymous letter, and by certain people, that someone in the neighbourhood recently gave birth to a child.

I thought it right to call certain persons in this neighbourhood to testify, who may or may not have circulated such rumours, because it was right that anyone who is accused should know of the report being made against them, and also in order that they should have opportunity of denying and disputing the charge, and if guilty, it should be brought home to them.

With that, the inquest jury was dismissed.

They returned after just fifteen minutes deliberation to return a verdict of, 'Wilful murder against some person or persons unknown.' The inquest itself had lasted seven hours.

However, an inquest is not a trial (in which the burden of proof is far higher). There seems to have been insufficient evidence against Emma Hallett to mount a prosecution or even an arrest. She never faced a court trial for the alleged murder of her new-born child.

However, the court of public opinion weighed heavily against her in Rockbeare. Within a few years the 48-year-old appears to have been living alone in the village and calling herself a 'widow', although there seems to be some evidence to suggest that her husband, William, had in fact emigrated to the Americas during the early 1900s.

Emma Hallett finally passed away during the early 1920s, still alone, and still living in Rockbeare.

Two questions remain, nevertheless. Did Emma Hallett become a mother again at the age of forty-eight and callously dispose of her child? Or was there some other explanation?

Firstly, the evidence of her neighbour and sister-in-law, Sarah Mortimore, cannot be totally relied upon since there was undoubtedly a feud behind the two families. Mrs Mortimore also appears to have gone to some considerable lengths to cause Emma Hallett a great deal of unpleasantness. Yet, other witnesses seem positive in their assertions that Mrs Hallett was an expectant mother, despite Dr Somers suggesting at the inquest that he did not think Emma Hallett had delivered a child in recent weeks.

Emma Hallett always (perhaps unsurprisingly) maintained her innocence. Punishments for infanticide were harsh during the Victorian era. Had she been found guilty, Emma

Hallett would have received no social services support, no mental health assessment – other than perhaps being placed in Exeter Lunatic Asylum, no counselling, no therapy, and very little understanding. Instead, she might have expected a lengthy prison sentence, including hard labour.

Therefore, it is unsurprising that many Victorian women avoided the social stigma attached to unwanted pregnancies (particularly those out of wedlock), by concealing both their condition and the birth itself. Together with the financial burden, the possible emotional trauma and the physical health risks associated with becoming pregnant comparatively late in life, as in the case of Emma Hallett, many desperate and expectant women often surreptitiously sought out a dark and shameful service which mushroomed during the Victorian era.

Perhaps Emma Hallett was not guilty of murder after all, but instead an innocent victim of one of Devon or Dorset's many reprehensible 'baby farmers'?

In the next chapter, *The Angel Makers,* the vile women who plied this trade are revealed.

THE ANGEL MAKERS

There can be few darker and distressing practices to have emerged in Victorian society than that of baby farming. Although this, at that time, perfectly legal service began in the more populous cities, by the late Victorian era baby farming had spread to rural areas like Devon and Dorset. The advent of the railway network brought wealthy families out of the cities and into the shires, and with them came young female domestic staff. In an era without effective contraception, no regulation of adoption, no social services, no affordable healthcare, and no unemployment benefit, a young woman who became pregnant out of wedlock could expect instant dismissal, social disgrace, and little prospect of finding a husband or further employment. Even for older women, such as Emma Hallett who featured in the previous story, *Tragedy in Silver Lane*, the health and financial risks of an unplanned child might be severe.

With no support or sympathy from the state, a chance to prey on the misery of others presented itself to some unscrupulous women. Slowly but surely, via word of mouth and through a series of newspaper advertisements, untrained 'nurses' offered, what appeared to be, perfectly plausible fostering and adoption services to unmarried mothers.

The new mother would pay a fee, usually between £10 and £15 (today's equivalent of more than £1,000) to the 'nurse' in the hope that their child might be temporarily looked after or found a permanent foster home. Many of these naively optimistic young women even hoped that they might one day be able to reclaim their child. 'Baby farming', as it became known, soon became a lucrative business. Many 'nurses' offering this service went as far as placing seemingly legitimate advertisements in the Devon and Dorset press, pretending to be a God-fearing, childless, middle-class couple, in search of a child to adopt. Desperate unmarried mothers in their droves answered apparently reputable advertisements like these from the *Dorset County Chronicle* and the *Western Times*:

WANTED, by a Respectable Married Couple, Child to Adopt or Nurse; premium required – apply newspaper office.

WANTED: Respectable Married Woman wishes a baby to Nurse or Adopt. References. Apply in writing to 'Baby, Newspaper Office.'

WANTED: by respectable married couple, child to adopt; from birth preferred, premium £15.

WIDOW wishes baby girl to adopt, 3 to 9 months old; must be perfectly healthy; pretty preferred – apply news office.

The newspapers featured scores of such advertisements every single week, without any verification. Just how many of these listings were legitimate will never be known. Sadly, the practice of baby farming, and advertising for adoption, grew unchecked.

Although the practice seems cruel and callous to our modern sensibilities, many Victorian women had no practical alternative and welcomed the service. Passing the child to a 'baby farmer' had several obvious advantages - it was simple, legal, and could be arranged quickly - with very few questions asked. Abortion was illegal and, although back street terminations were offered by unscrupulous practitioners, they were a high-risk alternative, often resulting in, at best, failure, or, at worst, severe haemorrhaging and infection, criminal prosecution, or even death. Abandonment of the child by its mother was similarly illegal, with little sympathy or mental health support extended by the authorities to anyone found abandoning or disposing of their child. Selina Wadge became one of the first women to be hanged for such a crime at Bodmin Jail in 1878. As she faced the hangman's noose, Selina Wadge whispered the words, 'Lord deliver me from this miserable world.'

Whilst there were undoubtedly some warm-hearted 'nurses' who genuinely attempted to look after the children left in their charge, a significant minority were not. Many soon realised it was far more profitable to simply dispose of an unwanted baby. After all, murder yielded a far quicker and easier profit, with no need to spend weeks and months caring for another woman's child. The loss of yet another child was unlikely to attract attention, especially in an era when the infant mortality rate meant that a fifth of all children died before reaching their first birthday.

And, even if a mother tried to reclaim her baby, only to find the child had disappeared, she would often be too frightened or humiliated to inform the police, for fear of dismissal or prosecution.

Returning to the story of Emma Hallett from Rocksbeare. The weight of evidence seemed to weigh against the 48-year-old Emma, certainly the inquest jury believed that she had given birth and then murdered her newly born baby. However, perhaps the despairing Emma Hallett had instead sought out the services of a baby farmer? There were a number known to be operating in Devon and Dorset between 1870-1900, including, perhaps, the most notorious one of all.

As early as 1875 Devon magistrates were known to be investigating an elderly woman by the name of Betsy Benmore, who ran a baby farm in an isolated farm cottage outside Exmouth. A girl in domestic service, named Isobel Phillips, who did not wish her employers to know she had given birth, handed over her daughter Margaret to Betsy Benmore. According to the testimony of two doctors from the Royal Devon and Exeter Hospital, who were requested to call on the baby farmer by the distraught mother:

The fine healthy child had pined away and died of sheer starvation. During our visit we witnessed two other infants also living in the cottage, both excessively emaciated, and four other children and adults, and for them all, a pennyworth of milk was purchased daily.

Betsy Benmore was a registered pauper in receipt of one-shilling and sixpence per week in outdoor poor relief; and no doubt took in unwanted babies to supplement her meagre income. Despite three infants having died at her establishment during the previous twelve months, no action had yet been taken against her. Although too late for young Margaret Phillips, justice was at last served on Betsy Benmore, who was sentenced to twelve years penal servitude at Exeter Assizes in March 1875.

Another woman, using the name 'Mrs Cook', advertised her 'Nursing Services' at workhouses throughout Devon during the 1880s. At an inquest in December 1884, she was 'severely reprimanded' over the death of a baby left in her care. 'Mrs Cook' had received half-a-crown a week from the child's mother to care for the baby, on the understanding that the mother might reclaim her in the future. Unfortunately, as Dr Pearce stated at the inquest:

The child has been fed only on bread and water, sweetened with sugar. It is my opinion that the child died from want of proper food.

The coroner added:

This district is a great one for baby farming and it is time the matter received more attention. I have on previous occasions warned Mrs Cook, and other baby farmers, as to their conduct, but it appears to have served no purpose, and it is high time further steps were taken. I have no hesitation in saying that the way baby farming is being conducted in this county is nothing more than a legalised way of murdering children.

Even though 'Mrs Cook' was severely reprimanded by the authorities, she was not punished and presumably continued to operate as before, most probably under yet another pseudonym.

Not all 'nurses' offering their services were elderly or destitute, however. A seemingly respectable, and previously affluent, baby farmer operating in East Devon during the late 1880s, was eventually brought to justice.

Three years after the death of Emma Hallett's baby in Rockbeare, Alice Laura Hockley finally received the justice she deserved at the Devon Assizes in Exeter.

Thirty-year-old Alice pleaded guilty to the charge of neglect and manslaughter of Frederick Mashford, a two-year-old left in her 'care'. Alice Hockley begged for mercy from the jury, explaining that she was the daughter of a wealthy Royal Navy captain who had passed away, leaving her £4,400 (almost £700,000 today). She claimed to have lost the entire sum after investing in a drapery business which fell into bankruptcy shortly afterwards. Only then, to escape the workhouse and destitution, did she 'take in children to care, which I looked after as best I could.'

Nevertheless, her true character was revealed after the death of Frederick Mashford. The boy's mother had handed over her son to Alice Hockley in 1890 and agreed to pay four shillings a week for her son's care. At that time, he weighed thirty-eight pounds. Yet, by early 1892, at the age of sixteen months, Frederick weighed only eleven pounds and was removed by the mother. Sadly, he died shortly afterwards. An examination revealed he had also suffered two fractured arms and a broken hip. The child had never been treated by a doctor.

Alice Hockley was sentenced to twelve years' penal servitude in 1892, with the judge commenting on her 'evil character' and 'gross cruelty to the deceased'. It was also believed she may have agreed to take in many other children who were now missing.

Despite these truly awful cases, baby farming continued well into the twentieth century. it would be many years until Parliament finally passed a series of acts to better protect babies and young children. The *Infant Life Protection Act 1897* and later the *Children's Act 1908* included stipulations ensuring that the local authority be notified within forty-eight hours of 'any change of custody or death of a child aged under seven.' Council authorities were empowered to close any reported baby farms, or to enter homes suspected of abusing children and remove children to a place of safety. Most importantly, the duties of a childcare nurse were clearly laid defined in law: 'no infant could be kept by an unfit nurse who threatened, by neglect or abuse, its proper care and maintenance.'

However, despite this improvement in legislation, another notorious case outraged the county of Dorset in 1904, bringing with it a unique medical first for the region.

At the Dorset Assizes in Dorchester on Wednesday 8th June 1904 the county's population was shocked to learn that, despite new legislation and the dawn of the seemingly more enlightened Edwardian era, the themes explored in Thomas Hardy's controversial recent novel *Jude the Obscure* still dictated the behaviour of the under privileged. The expected role of women in society, attitudes to marriage, and the fear of ostracisation was still forcing women into the clutches of baby farmers.

A domestic servant from West Bay, Bessie Jackson, entrusted her illegitimate twin daughters, Dorothy and Ethel, together with her elder child, into the care of a widow named Emma Hooper, who lived in the village of Stoborough, between Wareham and Corfe Castle.

Bessie Jackson paid Emma Hooper a total of two pounds and six shillings a month (approximately £300 today, and probably the majority of her income) for the care of her three children. Bessie was in domestic service at the time and knew that if her employers had discovered she had given birth out of wedlock, she would face instant dismissal without a reference and thus with little chance of obtaining another position. The first opportunity for Bessie to visit her children in Emma Hooper's care came on 9th May 1904, and she was horrified at the sight that confronted her as she walked through the door of the cottage in Stoborough.

Bessie called the local police, who immediately arrested Emma Hooper. An examination of the children was ordered using a pioneering new technology known as Röntgen Rays, named after the German physicist Wilhelm Röntgen. Whilst working in his laboratory in 1895, Röntgen had detected electromagnetic radiation in a wavelength range which he dubbed 'X-rays', after the mathematical symbol 'X', meaning the unknown. Six weeks later he took a radiograph image of his wife's hand which revealed her skeleton. In shock, she exclaimed, 'I have seen my death!'. In honour of his accomplishment Röntgen would receive the inaugural Nobel Prize for Physics in 1901.

The new technology was first accepted in a criminal trial in the USA during 1896, in which an image of a shotgun wound was displayed for the benefit of the jury. Although the radiograph from a Röntgen Ray had been used in a civil injury lawsuit in 1902 by Dr Percy Stirk from the Royal Devon and Exeter Hospital, its utilisation in the case against Emma Hooper may well have been the first use of X-rays in a successful British criminal trial. The images gathered by the Röntgen Rays (as they were still labelled by the newspapers at that time) were able to prove

that the children had suffered horrific abuse at the hands
of the baby farmer. The tragic case was reported in the
Bournemouth Daily Echo:

The evidence for the prosecution disclosed gross neglect and ill-usage.
A box filled with straw served as a cradle, and the children were never
taken out into the fresh air. When discovered on May 9th they were
much emaciated. The Rontgen rays revealed that the right shoulder
blade of the child Dorothy and both the bones of her legs had been
fractured. The broken ends of the bones had grown together irregularly
without surgical aid. The prisoner, Emma Hooper, at the time, said to
the Inspector, 'If I had called a doctor, I should have had to pay him.'
The prisoner was sentenced to twelve months' hard labour, the Judge
describing it as a truly dreadful case.

Returning to the case of Emma Hallett from the village
of Rocksbeare, it is certainly possible that she did not
murder her child, but instead employed the services of a
baby farmer, or answered one of the many advertisements
placed in the local press by 'nurses' posing as married
couples seeking a child to adopt. For a mother to murder
her own baby and then dispose of the body within a few
hundred yards of her own house, seems far harder to
believe, than the possibility that she actively sought the
help of an unofficial (but seemingly plausible) adoption
service. Remember, Emma Hallett had travelled to North
Devon for several days prior to the arrival of her baby;
conceivably she had arranged for a baby farmer to collect
her child following its birth? She was, after all, noted by
her neighbours as 'appearing to be very weak'. Perhaps she
had persuaded a 'nurse' to collect the newly born child for
a small fee, only for the unscrupulous baby farmer to wait
until the hours of darkness and then dispose of the baby's

body in the pond between Silver Lane and Rocksbeare Manor.

Surely, though, not even by the low standards set by the most ruthless of Victorian baby farmers, such callous behaviour could not be imagined?

Step forward the most notorious and heartless baby farmer of all, the infamous Amelia Dyer.

MRS DYER.
(From Police Pictures.)

Born in Bristol in 1837, Dyer had trained as a nurse, and knew the West Country well. Operating under many aliases, she took to baby farming following the death of her husband in 1869.
She frequently admitted herself to mental asylums at times which coincided with the disappearance of children in her care; and she felt it convenient to 'disappear'. Dyer even committed herself into the care of the Somerset and Bath Lunatic Asylum near Wells, shortly after the discovery of Emma Hallett's child. As a former nurse, Amelia Dyer knew exactly how to conduct herself, thus ensuring a relatively comfortable life as an asylum inmate.

She was eventually arrested in London, just as she planned to return to Somerset and disappear again, following the suspicions of a London doctor which had been reported to the police. Dyer was tried for the murder of just one child, Doris Marmon; she was, however, suspected to have killed between 300-400 babies over many decades, making her probably the most prolific serial killer in British history. Amelia Dyer was executed on 10ᵗʰ June 1896, taking the secret of the true number of children murdered by her to the grave.

During the investigation into her actions, police discovered dressmaking equipment, including white tape used to kill the children in her care (similar to the stay lace used on the body of Emma Hallett's child).

Two years after Amelia Dyer's execution, railway workers at Newton Abbot station in Devon found a parcel hidden in a carriage. Inside the parcel was a three-week-old baby girl. Although cold and wet, she was miraculously still alive. The baby had been entrusted to a lady calling herself 'Mrs Stewart', for a fee of £12. 'Mrs Stewart' had picked up the baby at Plymouth railway station, then cruelly abandoned her on the very next train. 'Mrs. Stewart' was thought by police to be Polly, the daughter of Amelia Dyer.

It is certainly possible that poor Emma Hallett was yet another victim of Amelia Dyer, or another of the many unscrupulous baby farmers known to have been acting in Devon and Dorset at the time. Perhaps an injustice was done to Emma Hallett, who may have been yet another victim of this horrific trade. We will never know.

Sadly, the wheels of justice turned slowly in Victorian England. Only when adoption services became officially regulated, beginning with the *Children's Act 1908*, did the baby farmers eventually cease to ply their callous trade. Too late for the many babies and grief-stricken mothers, silently suffering among the bustling population of Devon and Dorset.

STORM IN A TEACUP

In January 1934, six young 'door-to-door' travelling salesmen and saleswomen (as they were then called) arrived in Dorchester. The group took temporary lodging in the town, giving their names as Abraham Levine, (nineteen-years-old and the manager of the group) Leah Levine (his sister), Gerald Serf, Dennis Reginald McGuigan, Geoffrey Thomas Osborne, and Annie Miller. They gave their employers as Messrs Lovett & Sons Tea Importers, 23a Commercial Road, Southampton. Their names were genuine, as was their business address. However, little else of their story was true.

The group of six was intent on continuing their hugely lucrative, but highly questionable, sales scheme, from which they had each already made a sizeable profit. This time, the housewives of Dorchester were to be the target. Their cleverly planned scheme was technically legal, if somewhat dubious. With several layers of management involved, it would prove difficult for the authorities to apportion blame, meaning any threat of legal action against the six individuals would amount to little more than a storm in a teacup. However, if the police could prove that the scheme was fraudulent, then trouble might be brewing for the sharp practising group.

The group carefully selected various Dorchester addresses to target as part of their elaborate plan. They utilised the following criteria when selecting suitable targets for the scheme:

1) Properties at which they thought it likely that the housewife would be home alone, or perhaps a widow.

2) Homes from which the husband would be safely away at work.

3) Houses at which it appeared to be 'washing day', the day on which housewives were usually at their busiest and most likely to be easy targets.

Lawyers and the police during the 1920s and '30s, often referred to housewives being dupped by the sharp practices of door-to-door salesmen as having made a 'washing day mistake.'

At the 22 different homes targeted in Dorchester an identical tactic was always used. The first housewife to receive a knock on the door was Mrs Florence Jolliffe of Dagmar Road in the town:

Good morning, madam, was the greeting Mrs Jolliffe received as she opened the door to Dennis McGuigan (one of the six-strong sales team), *I've got some great news for you. You are one of only twelve lucky people to have been selected in Dorchester, who will receive a special gift.*

Already flattered and disarmed, Florence Jolliffe enquired, *What special gift?*

If you buy one pound of our finest tea, you will receive £3 in a week's time, McGuigan announced (£3 equates to approximately £280 today).

How can you afford to do that? Mrs Jolliffe enquired.

We are blending tea to suit the Dorchester water. The gifts are an advertising scheme, for the first twelve customers, and you are one of the lucky ones.

That's a lot of money to spend on tea, though.

Ah, but our tea is the finest choice blended tea, from Ridgways of London. We offer Indian, Ceylon, China, Golden Tips, or Digestive Tea.

Suitability impressed, Mrs Jolliffe purchased one pound of tea and McGuigan promised to return the following week, to collect another order, and with a guarantee promising the £3 gift (although, not the actual money).

And so, the scheme continued. Next, the sales agents called at Mrs Sheppick's house in Cambridge Road, then Mrs Loder, Mrs Player, Mrs Lock in Dagmar Road, and many, many more. Sometimes, if the householder seemed hesitant, the agents would reduce the minimum purchase of tea to half a pound, with a £1 reward to be paid in a few weeks' time. On every occasion, the premium quality of the tea being supplied was assured.

After a week had passed, the sales agents returned to all the addresses and attempted to sell the housewives another pound of tea. No agent called on the same house twice. Each week, the agent feigned ignorance regarding what the housewife had been told by the previous caller. Mrs Pattle in Louise Road was informed:

No, Mrs Pattle, I don't know what the other salesman told you, but in a month you get a guarantee for £3. You were busy last week, perhaps you misunderstood. But the money is guaranteed.

Mrs Hawkins in Dagmar Road snapped at the sales agent, *Mr Osborne, I see from this guarantee I have to wait eleven months for the money. I understood it would come after a month.*

Thomas Osborne replied, *You might get it any time, Mrs Hawkins, or you might not have it until after this date.* He pointed to the printed guarantee he had handed her, on which had been printed 'January 14th 1935', a full twelve months away, *And, to get the £3, you will be expected to buy a pound of tea each week.*

Mrs Pidden, also from Dagmar Road, also stirred the pot a little more,

There's some catch in it, there must be.

God's honour, woman. There's no catch.

Well, I've never put such muck in my teapot before! She added.

All the Dorchester housewives agreed that the tea was of a very poor quality, referring to it as 'Java tea'. Today, Java tea is recognised for its herbal and medicinal qualities. However, when Java tea first arrived on British shores from the Dutch colonies during the early part of the twentieth century, it was generally thought to be of an inferior quality; not being an 'Empire tea'.

Nevertheless, the six sales agents pressed on, becoming more forceful with their prospective customers. When the elderly Mrs Player in Dagmar Road told one of the salesmen, Gerald Serf, that she couldn't afford to buy a pound of tea as she was an old age pensioner, he persuaded her to buy half a pound a week instead. Once he had obtained the order, he left the house, leaving Mrs Player in tears. Fortunately for the tea drinking population of Dorchester, Mrs Jolliffe was one step ahead of the high-pressure sales agents.

When Gerald Serf knocked on her front door in Dagmar Road again, on 29ᵗʰ January, her husband was waiting in the hallway, out of sight of Serf. Alfred Jolliffe was an ex-police sergeant and railway security guard, and fully prepared to take whatever action was necessary. Gerald Serf was greeted by Mrs Jolliffe:

Good morning, Mrs Jolliffe.

Morning. Do you have my £3?

No, but I have your guarantee here. This document means you will receive your money very soon.

How soon? My husband and me, need the money now.

Well, you have to keep buying our tea to get the reward.

Mr Jolliffe suddenly leapt out from behind the door, *We've had this tea tasted by someone, and it's not worth sixpence a pound, let alone what you're charging!*

Gerald Serf was taken aback, but quickly regained his composure, *Then you won't want any more of our tea, then.*

He turned and promptly walked back up the garden path to the gate. Mr Jolliffe shouted after him, *Just a minute, you. We've reported the whole thing to the police superintendent.*

Have you!

Yes, replied the former policeman, grabbing Serf's arm as the much younger man attempted to hurry away down the street. Meanwhile, the residents of Dagmar Road looked out incredulously on the commotion. The quiet and pleasant road of red brick terraced houses was clearly not used to such goings on! Serf struggled free and ran away in the direction of Alexandra Road, shouting back as he did so: *You can't read! The money is guaranteed!*

The population of Dorset has always possessed a sense of justice and fair play, perhaps unrivalled anywhere else in the land. This was highlighted by the courageous and self-sacrificing stand of the downtrodden agrarian classes against the government's Trade Union legislation, in the form of the Tolpuddle Martyrs, the Milton Abbas Martyrs, the Bridport Bread Rioters - frustrated by the unfair nature of the Corn Laws, the anti-reformers during the General Elections of 1831 and 1862, and the burning of hayricks as part of the Swing Riots. To deny an Englishman a good cup of tea, and to play unfairly into the bargain, seems to have raised the sense of injustice to boiling point.

The guarantee forms issued to the housewives were handed over to the Dorchester police and an investigation demanded. Fortunately, the forms displayed the company's address in Southampton - 23a Commercial Road - making the sales agents relatively easy to trace. A warrant was issued, and a series of arrests soon followed.

The six sales agents were then charged as follows:

Abraham Levine, a tea merchant of Upper Street, Islington, London, Gerald Serf, of East India Dock Road, Dennis Reginald McGuigan, of Bedford Place, Southampton, Geoffrey Thomas Osborne, of Carlisle Road, Shirley, Southampton, Leah Levine, sister of Abraham, and Annie Miller of Ashley Road, Birmingham, you are charged with conspiring to defraud a number of Dorchester housewives in regard to the sale of tea.

All six pleaded 'Not guilty' and the case was pushed forward, with remarkable speed, to be heard at the Dorset Quarter Assizes on 17th February.

Meanwhile, the housewives were not idle. Letters were written to local newspapers across the country, in case the sales agents had attempted the same sharp practice elsewhere:

Sir

Would you allow me space in your valuable paper to put housewives on their guard against 'tea frauds'.

Nearly a fortnight ago two women called at my house and said that my name had been sent to them from their manager as I was a needy case (being a widow), and if I purchased 1lb of tea at 3s 2d, I would receive £2 5s the following week, out of which I would be expected to buy another 2lb of tea.

I refused, but they asked if I could borrow or raise 3 s 2d somehow, as they wanted me to get this £2 5s gift, me being so hard up It happened that a neighbour of mine came in, and she suggested going halves, as their tale convinced her, and so we purchased 1lb of tea. They promised to be back with their manager the following week, but needless to say, we have been hoaxed.

Perhaps they will try it on with some other poor person like myself, hence my letter of warning.

TAKEN-IN

There was great interest in Dorchester as the trial date arrived. With intense public scrutiny, the Crown retained the services of JG Trapnell, KC, and JM Walker KC The appointed defence barrister was to be Charles Garfield Lott Du Cann, an outspoken, expensive and notorious KC who had also penned several books including the controversial *The Young Person's Complete Guide to Crime*. The prosecution team was given a clue as to the depth and scale of the bonus tea fraudsters, when it was announced that the defence had been instructed by one of London's leading law firms, Courts & Co. It was also felt important enough to point out by the *Western Gazette*'s reporter, that the jury contained two women, of whom it was felt would better understand the importance of the charge.

Mr Trapnell opened the prosecution's case:

Ladies and gentlemen of the jury, we aim to prove, in substance, a charge of conspiracy to sell to people in this district, tea which is little more than worthless. In fact, not good tea at all, and to attempt to sell it by certain representations, tricks to induce people, and thus deceive them.

He continued, outlining the circumstances of the alleged scheme and attempting to show the dubious nature of the enterprise:

It appears that Abraham Levine signed an agreement to take some premises in Southampton which consisted of only a small room with a table and three or four chairs, in a name which was not his own. It appears that these premises were never, in fact, occupied.

The tea, which is still in its packets, and has been examined by experts, is not Indian, Ceylon, or China tea, but was Java tea, which has been described as rubbish, or stale tea.

*Furthermore, the guarantee which was posted through people's
letterboxes was in fact a nonsensical sort of document. It is printed
and bears no signature, and would be worthless in a Court of law,
even if it claimed to entitle the holder to just a penny piece. Although
these people had been told they would have their money in less than a
month or thereabouts, the actual expiring dates on the documents were
all in the year 1935.*

The case seemed fairly damning and the packed public
gallery shook their heads with disapproval, as if watching
the evidence unfold in a gruesome murder trial.

The expert witness, from Tizard Tea and
Coffee Specialists of Dorchester, gave his
opinion on the tea, stating that it was,
'Not good. Quite dead and should have
been destroyed.' Mr Du Cann bitterly
objected to the witness, claiming that, as
a Dorchester tea supplier, Tizard's had
a conflict of interest, and that Abraham
Levine should not be prosecuted, since he
could not be blamed for the actions of his

sales agents. However, this was overruled. Abraham Levine
was then questioned at some length by his own defence
barrister.

Du Cann, *Where did you get the tea?*

Levine, *From Ridgways, Above Bar, Southampton. I paid cash for it.*

Du Cann, *What sort of tea did you buy?*

Levine, *I asked for a cheap, decent, drinkable brand.*

Mr Du Cann then produced several receipts for £250
worth of tea (£23,000 today) and noted that the tea was

labelled as 'special' or 'specially packed', costing around one shilling and a halfpenny a pound.

Du Cann, *Although you have been selling tea since you were sixteen, did you know anything about it at all?*

Levine, *I know nothing at all about the quality of tea. Ridgways are a reputable firm. They are one of the best known in the country. I thought I was carrying on an honest business. In fact, if this case hadn't happened, I would have been able to pay the customers their gift of £3 under the scheme.*

Du Cann, *You are selling at a high price, but there is no law against that.*

Levine nodded his head in agreement.

Du Cann, *You were carrying on a big business for a boy of nineteen?*

Levine, *There's no law against that either.*

In total, twenty-two housewives from Dorchester gave evidence in a trial lasting five hours. For the prosecution, Mr Trapnell told the jury that Levine and his team, 'had put forward a scheme with a good deal of guile. Yet there was a deliberate attempt to mislead the customer.'

Mr Du Cann, for the defence, opened his speech by stating:

I want to dispose of some of the fog of prejudice that surrounds my case. Whether you are a Dorchester jury or an English jury, you have taken an oath to give a verdict according to the evidence and not according to your local prejudice, or local ideas.

He was severely reprimanded at this point, and threw down his papers in disgust, before continuing:

It seems what I was told was correct! But what is this case about? It amounts to a few pounds of tea. Gift schemes are advertised every day. This is little more than the case of an ambitious young man using a few tricks of the trade.

The jury were sent away to consider their verdict on three charges. After more than an hour they returned, finding the defendants 'Not guilty' of selling inferior quality tea, by representing it as a choice brand. They were, however, found guilty of conspiring to defraud the housewives by mentioning a reward of £3, and on a further charge of general charge of conspiring to defraud. Abraham Levine and Dennis McGuigan were sentenced to three months' imprisonment, Leah Levine to one month, and the remaining sales agents were fined £20 and bound over for one year.

Although the sentences may seem a little harsh, the true scale of the scheme came to light after the trial, thanks to the determination of a handful of Dorchester housewives and the publicity campaign they organised. Abraham and Leah Levine had no less than thirty-four previous convictions each, for obtaining money by false pretences. In fact, 'Bonus Tea Schemes' had been presented to the unsuspecting British public in many areas of the country, and involving a huge number of pyramid sellers, of which Levine and his team were just one. Unfortunately, as the majority of victims were too embarrassed to report the crime, or felt the matter too trivial, stories of the tea schemes were generally only reported locally. However, the Dorchester 'Teapot Martyrs' brought the scheme into national focus and stories of similar schemes were reported from Kilmarnock, Kirkcaldy, Glasgow and Perth in Scotland; and from Burnley, Lincoln, London, Bromley and Ilfracombe in England.

Despite several high-profile arrests during the 1930s, and many more prosecutions, the schemes continued for many years, even prompting the *Daily Mirror* to join the campaign for 'Housewives' Justice':

GRATEFUL BRITISH HOUSEWIVES
support the Daily Mirror*'s Campaign Against Tea-Bonus Frauds*

The Daily Mirror's *campaign against the bogus bonus tea pushers is growing in support. Our exposure of the Bonus-Tea Concerns is creating the greatest of interest, says the editor. In our next issue we will be adding to this powerful campaign, by assisting the genuine trader to uphold his position in face of heavy rents, taxes and other charges. We have received the gratitude of thousands of housewives for our ruthless exposure of the Bonus-Tea frauds. The names of four new bonus-tea firms have been submitted by* Daily Mirror *readers. They are: The Continental Tea Stores, The Crown Tea Company, Stanley's Tea Stores, and W Levine and Co. These firms offer bonuses ranging from £6 to £1 to customers who take their tea regularly. The* Daily Mirror *repeats its advice to housewives not to have anything to do with firms selling tea on the bonus baits.*

The last reported prosecution took place in Leicester in 1939. However, after the introduction of rationing and heavy penalties for profiteering during the Second World War, the schemes disappeared and are largely forgotten today. Nevertheless, without the efforts of the Dorchester 'Teapot Martyrs' there may have been many more British housewives stirring inferior tea in their teapots, anxiously waiting for a bonus of £3.

WHEN IS MURDER, MURDER?
(PART ONE)

To indulge one's instinctive and uncontrolled sense of justice and right, was not, he had found, permitted with impunity in an old civilization like ours

Thomas Hardy, *Jude the Obscure*, 1895

On Friday 16th November 1877, the *Bridport News* published a withering diatribe in which it bemoaned the failure of the legal system to correctly bring the murderer of a policeman to justice. In fact, the killing of police constable Thomas Bishop, two months earlier, in Bere Regis on Thursday 20th September, had been the second murder of a serving police constable within a twelve-month period. Both crimes caused a national outcry, which was lucidly expressed by the editor of the *Bridport News*:

In the eyes of the law—or rather those who administer it—a policeman's life is evidently of not so much value as an ordinary person's. We began to form this opinion when we learned the result of the trial of the Hutchings family for the murder of PC Cox last year in Yeovil; and now the issue of proceedings against Henry Lock, for the murder PC Bishop, at Bere Regis, near Wareham, confirms that impression.

Those intending to be policemen would do well to remember this. We shall always hold that to murder a man who is carrying out the law is the most heinous of crimes, for he is risking his life for the good of the general community. If to kill one of the ordinary public is murder, we should say that to kill one who is endeavouring to preserve the peace and comfort of the public is the worst phase of that crime.

Surely, among the ruffians of the country, in fact, looking at it from a criminal's point of view, it may be said that the criminal has had his money's worth. Such lenient treatment of man-slayers, which acts as a dampener on the praiseworthy zeal of the consistent policeman, is a cause for great chuckling among the roughs throughout the land. The value of the police force is materially lessened by too much licence being allowed to the lawless subject.

Viewed now, with the perspective of time and distance, the sentence meted out to the offender in this story seems extraordinarily lenient. It appears that justice in 1877 was highly selective. For example, an unmarried woman might face dismissal from her position, or worse, for becoming pregnant. A married woman could not own property, it belonged to her husband. A child of ten might be legitimately employed for up to ten hours a day. A working man could, at last, choose to join a trade union, but he still might expect to be treated harshly should he decide to strike for better pay.

Yet, nineteenth century courts seemed strangely lenient, when applying the law to the drinking habits of the working man. Victorian society frequently appeared prepared to excuse almost endless violence, when alcohol acted as a contributing factor.

Thursday 20th September 1877 had been the day of the

Woodbury Hill Fair and a large number of both visitors
and locals had gathered in the Drax Arms in the usually
quiet village of Bere Regis, near Wareham. As 'drinking
up' time approached, a dozen or so noisy and inebriated
individuals spilled out of the public house and onto Bere
Street (now West Street). Two local constables, PC Thomas
Bishop and PC John Sansom, had been charged with
keeping public order and persuading the rowdy crowd
to make their way home. Constable Bishop was aged
thirty-eight with many years' experience in the Dorset
Constabulary. Although considered a lenient and patient
man, he had already endured several previous altercations
with a local man, Henry Lock, a twenty-two-year-old
labourer, who seemed to be the noisiest of those now
shouting and singing outside the Drax Arms.

Opposite the public house was an entrance leading into an
enclosed space known locally as Wenell's Yard, in which
there were three small cottages; one of which was occupied

by Henry Lock and his father. The cottages could be reached through two separate gated pathways, one at either end of the yard.

Seeing Henry Lock shouting and generally behaving abusively, PC Bishop said to him, 'Henry, make no noise, but go home.'

Those gathered around thought that the constable's manner was tolerant and not at all heavy-handed. However, Henry Lock ignored him and continued to shout. He was asked again to 'go home', and this time he did start to walk along the pathway leading to his father's cottage. Knowing Lock's previous character, and to ensure that he really did go home (and not just exit Wenell's Yard again by the back entrance), PC Bishop escorted Lock to the door of his cottage. As they approached the door, Henry Lock became more and more violent, resisting the constable. On hearing the melee, a small group began shouting, and tried to follow the two men into the yard. PC Sansom remained at the gateway into the yard, while PC Bishop drew his stick, as a struggle ensued between himself and Henry Lock. The policeman lashed out at Lock with his stick and Lock retaliated with his fists. Noticing a lantern still burning inside the cottage window, PC Bishop shouted up to Henry's father, 'Thomas Lock, take in your son now!'

Receiving no answer, he repeated the request. As he did so, Henry Lock stopped resisting. Thinking that the altercation was at an end, PC Bishop told Lock to go to bed; then turned and started to walk back to the street. As he did so, Lock picked up a large and heavy piece of flint from the border of the flowerbed and hurled it violently at the constable. Bishop was only a few yards away when the three-pound lump of flint struck him on the left side of the head, just above his right ear. He collapsed to the ground in an instant and lay there, unmoving. Lock stood over the motionless policeman and threw another stone which again struck PC Bishop on the head. One of the bystanders, Frederick Ricketts, a local shoemaker, rushed forward and attempted to help the motionless policeman, carefully trying to pick PC Bishop up from the ground. As he did so, Henry Lock snarled, 'If you pick him up, I'll knock the bastard down again!'

Frederick Ricketts ignored Lock's angry instruction and gathered up the semi-conscious policeman. Furiously, Lock rained down a punch with such force that it knocked the constable out of Ricketts's grasp and back onto the ground. He then continued his assault on the policeman's limp body while Fredrick Ricketts grabbed him around the waist and attempted to pull him away.

Eventually, Ricketts was able to push Lock inside his cottage and then rushed to fetch help. He reached PC Sansom first and cried out, 'Come quick! Your mate is beaten bad.'

Dr Lys was immediately sent for, and PC Bishop was carried home, where the doctor attended to him throughout the night. Having suffered a four-inch fracture on the left side of his skull, two black eyes, heavy bruising on the nose, left cheek, on each temple, and on both arms, the constable was pronounced dead at 5.30am.

Henry Lock was arrested at his father's cottage within an hour of the assault. On being apprehended and charged with murder, Lock answered, 'I am not guilty, he badly treated me first.'

Lock was remanded in custody, while enquiries were made. In the meantime, it was thought judicious to have him examined by a doctor, to ascertain if there was any truth in his allegations of having been first assaulted by PC Bishop during the two men's altercation. However, despite Lock claiming that he had been savagely attacked by the constable, his body exhibited no injuries, with the exception of one small bruise on the back of his right hand.

Four days after the murderous attack, on Tuesday 20th September, the funeral of PC Thomas Bishop took place at St John's Church in Bere Regis. As a mark of respect, all the window blinds in the village were drawn and the village school and local shops closed. The funeral procession was led by a contingent of 24 fellow constables, the Chief Constable of Dorset, and virtually the entire population of the village. The Rev John Langford conducted the service in the recently renovated church and pleaded with the 300 strong congregation to 'lead a Christian life and not look forward to the end of your life merely as a rest from the sorrows, afflictions and trials you have endured.'

Meanwhile, according to the venomous Dorset press, Henry Lock did not seem to be reflecting on his own afflictions and trials, but positively 'enjoying' his incarceration in jail, where he, 'manifests but little concern at his position. He converses freely with the other prisoners, and eats and sleeps well, apparently troubling himself but little about the future.'

Following the funeral, Rev Langford rallied support for a collection on behalf of PC Bishop's widow and son, which raised more than £50 (a handsome sum, equivalent to more than £7,500 today). In 1877 the maximum official compensation granted to the widow of a policeman killed in the line of duty was £63 17s. 6d. Although at that time a policeman in Dorset might expect to receive a pension on retirement, this was not automatically transferred to his widow in the event of his death. The oversight would have left PC Bishop's widow penniless, had it not been for the local collection. The anomaly in the regulations was finally corrected in 1891; sadly, too late for the widow of Thomas Bishop to receive his pension.

An initial magistrates' hearing was held at Wareham Town Hall, overseen by Colonel Mansel and the Earl of Eldon, during which a scowling Henry Lock denied ever threatening PC Bishop. A verdict of 'Wilful Murder' was recorded against Lock, and the coroner formally declared that:

Thomas Bishop was, on 20ᵗʰ September, at Bere Regis, assaulted and beaten by Henry Lock, causing an effusion of blood from which injuries he died, and that Henry Lock did feloniously kill and slay Thomas Bishop.

After the inquest verdict was announced, Lock was hurriedly conveyed through the jostling crowd, then escorted, via the 5.30pm train to Dorchester, where he was remanded in the county jail.

A trial date was set for Thursday 8ᵗʰ November at the Winter Assizes in Winchester. Herbert Cary George Batten QC, from the famous Dorset legal family of Fairlee House on the Isle of Wight, prosecuted on behalf of the Crown. Henry Lock was defended by Mr Charles Matthew QC. Mr Justice Henry Lopes presided (Justice Lopes and

Charles Matthews also crossed swords in another story in this book, *The Whit Monday Murder*, which contains further detail about their colourful careers).

The trial opened and Henry Lock presented a haggard appearance as he was ushered into the dock. His eyes were red and inflamed, and it was evident that he now realised his precarious position. When asked to answer the indictment *of* 'wilfully murdering Police Constable Thomas Bishop', he fought back streams of tears as he sobbed out 'Not guilty' to the packed courtroom. He then leaned forward, appearing to concentrate intently, as HCG Batten began the case for the prosecution:

Gentleman of the jury, the facts of this case are clear. The deceased met his death at the hands of the prisoner, while in the execution of his duty. But the question was whether the prisoner's act amounted to the crime of murder with malice, or that of manslaughter.

Before continuing his opening address, Mr Batten first outlined the facts of the case for the jury, which caused an audible murmur of disapproval in the public gallery:

Those are the facts of the case, and it is for you, the jury, to attach to them the weight they deserve. The question is not so much whether the deceased came to his death by the violence of the prisoner, as to whether that violence would make the offence one of murder. I have no doubt my friend acting for the prisoner's defence, Mr Matthews, would strongly urge that it was only manslaughter. Nevertheless, when a man meets his death at the hands of another, it is murder; unless it can be shown that it was justifiable or excusable on account of provocation.

I need not occupy your time any further, before calling the witnesses to this horrific offence, other than to remind you, the jury, that after the prisoner had thrown the stone at the deceased man, and Constable Bishop had fallen to the ground, he went up to him, took another stone and threw it upon him, and then proceeded to beat him. All this went to show that there must have been malice – which is a definition of murder, over and above manslaughter.

Frederick Ricketts, the principal witness to the tragic events, was the first witness to be called. He carefully explained the circumstances leading up to PC Bishop's death:

Henry Lock and some other men were making a noise outside the Drax Arms. I saw Constable Bishop go towards Lock and speak to him. Lock went towards Wenell's Yard, and Bishop followed him and endeavoured to force him towards his own home. PC Sansom stopped at the entrance to the yard, to keep the crowd back. I went round near the blacksmith's shop and looked over. Bishop called out something, but I could not hear what. Bishop was flourishing his staff and Lock was squaring at the constable with his fists. I shouted to Lock, 'Do not strike him, if you do, you will be punished for it.' He immediately picked up a large stone and threw it, striking Bishop on the head with it. He threw another stone and afterwards struck Bishop with his fists.

I went to Bishop and said, 'You are very much hurt, Bishop, ain't you?' Bishop did not reply. After getting Lock indoors, I went to PC Sansom for assistance.

Charles Matthews was given the chance to cross-examine the witness on behalf of the defence:

Mr Ricketts, Wenell's Yard is a private one occupied in common by three tenants, Mrs Hall, Mr Lock, senior, and Mrs Byles. There are two entrances, one of them from Bere Street and the other from the Elder Road side. The gate was one which opened and closed…

Mr Matthews was abruptly interrupted by Mr Justice
Lopes:

*Mr Matthews, this does not seem much like a question for the witness,
but like the beginning of your defence. Do you have a question?*

I do, your honour. Several, in fact.

Then please ask them!

Suitably reprimanded, Charles Matthews continued, *Mr
Ricketts, might PC Bishop have drawn his staff before they entered the
yard?*

I cannot tell, sir, replied the witness.

And how long did their altercation last?

*I could not say whether the struggle lasted as long as ten minutes, but
I should think it did. Bishop had his helmet on when they entered the
yard, but it was knocked off before he turned to go back out.*

The next witness, PC Sansom, was then asked to testify:

*On the night in question there were twenty or thirty persons outside the
Drax Arms. Lock formed one of a party of about ten or a dozen. I
was a little way down the street but I heard someone, who appeared to
be Lock, commence making a noise, as though he was going to begin
making a disturbance. Bishop went up to him and said, 'You go home
quiet, now.' Lock moved away, but made more noise than before. Lock
said something about the police. Bishop then said to him, 'If you don't
go home quiet, I shall take you home.' Lock was continually making
a noise from the time he left the crowd till he got indoors. Bishop
followed him.*

Again, Charles Matthews cross-examined the witness:

Wenell's Yard was gravelled, PC Sansom, but was there blood about?

I could not swear that, sir, but there were marks of a severe struggle.

How do you know they were marks of a struggle, then, constable?

The ground was a little disturbed, and this led me to say there had been a struggle.

Mr Justice Lopes once again interrupted the defence's cross-examination. On this occasion, to clarify a point for the jury:

Gentlemen of the jury, it appears that Bishop told Lock to go home. He then followed him. We do not know what Bishop's reason was for following him. It appears that Lock never resisted the constable but, in fact, walked away from him.

Two further witnesses also provided a similar picture of the commotion outside the Drax Arms that night, before Mr Batten moved onto the events of the following morning. Sergeant James Hill had been given the task of arresting Henry Lock, and was given the opportunity to describe what happened when he arrived at Wenell's Yard:

I arrived at Lock's house at about midnight on the night of the 20th September. It is the middle cottage of three in the yard. I found the door locked. Lock's father came to the window and asked what I wanted, and I told him I wanted to speak to Henry. I then apprehended Henry Lock and charged him with violently assaulting Constable Bishop. On the way to the police station Lock said, 'I don't care for any bastard policeman. I'll fight Bishop again, even if he has got a staff.'

After he was taken to the police station, Lock complained of having been badly beaten with a policeman's staff. He was then examined by Dr Lys. The trousers and shirt he was then wearing had a quantity of blood on the trousers and both sleeves of the shirt were saturated with blood. His boots were spotted with blood and his hands and wrists were also covered.

At the police station I formally charged Henry Lock with the murder of PC Bishop. He said to me, 'Is he dead?'. I answered, 'He is'. He then said, 'Oh, then, it's a bad job.'

Then, in the light of morning, I went to Wenell's Yard and saw that one of the flints round the flower border, near Lock's door, had been recently taken out. There was blood on several of the stones, and another stone was missing from the border of Mrs Hall's garden plot. I found the stone, which has been shown here in evidence today. It had a quantity of blood on it, and it fitted the space in the flower border in every particular.

If the testimony in the trial so far appeared to have damaged Henry Lock's cause a great deal, then the evidence from the next three witnesses seemed to seal his fate. Surely, only a brilliant performance by his barrister could now save him from the gallows.

WHEN IS MURDER, MURDER?
(PART TWO)

And staring face to face,
I shot at him, as he at me,
And killed him in his place.

Thomas Hardy, *The Man He Killed*, 1902

The next witness to be called in the trial of Henry Lock
was Mrs Ann Biles, who occupied one of the other cottages
in Wenell's Yard, and also overheard the disturbance:

I heard a voice say 'Lock, take in your son', and then another voice
saying 'Lock, put down that stone'.

Another witness, Thomas Arnold, was then called to the
stand. He testified that, while drinking in the Drax Arms,
Henry Lock had said to him:

Thomas, that Bishop is always at me.

I will have him before Woodbury Hill Fair is done.

However, this damning piece of evidence seems to have
been slightly diluted by Thomas Arnold then claiming
that he had also seen PC Bishop share a drink with Henry
Lock in the passageway of the inn. This new piece of

information necessitated a short conversation between the two barristers and Justice Lopes, as this revelation appeared to contradict earlier testimony, in which it had been stated that PC Bishop had not been in the Drax Arms that evening. Nevertheless, Justice Lopes agreed to allow Thomas Arnold's evidence.

The next witness, James Hawker, a labourer, claimed he had overheard Henry Lock in the public house, expressing his hatred for the police. However, this time, Mr Justice Lopes ordered the jury to disregard that piece of testimony, informing them that:

The statement in question, which this witness alleges was made by the prisoner, was clearly expression of a hatred against the police as a body, rather than against PC Bishop as an individual. Please strike those remarks from the record.

Unfortunately for Henry Lock, the damage was already done. The tide in the case was clearly turning against him.

Next came two historic and damaging pieces of evidences from Charles Lacey, the clerk at the magistrates court in Wareham; which were allowed by Mr Justice Lopes to be entered as evidence. Firstly, that Henry Lock had been summoned for 'drunk and riotous behaviour' two years earlier, on 3rd August 1875, following evidence given by PC Bishop. In a mirror image of the current offence, Constable Bishop had instructed Henry Lock to go home. Lock had pretended to do so; but was then arrested later in another part of Bere Street. Lock was again convicted of the same offence, on 27th February 1877, and again by evidence given by PC Bishop. On this occasion he was overheard by a local farmer, Tom Scutt, saying, 'Bishop, I will do for you some day!'

Matters in the trial quickly became even worse for Henry
Lock. A month before the death of Constable Bishop,
on 14ᵗʰ August, an associate of Henry Lock's, a man by
the name of William Lockyer, had been arrested by PC
Bishop for 'relieving himself in the churchyard of St
John's Church, Bere Regis, and thereby committing an
act of public indecency.' During the fourteen-day term of
imprisonment imposed on William Lockyer, Henry Lock
visited him in the police cells. The two men's conversation
was overheard by Constable Edward Butler:

Constable Butler, Mr Batten asked, *Please tell the court, exactly
what you heard the prisoner say in that cell.*

*Yes, sir. He said 'If it hadn't been for that bastard Bishop, you would
not be here. I'll give him something if he don't look out.' Then, as he
left Lockyer, Lock yelled up from the yard, 'I'll do for the bastard if he
don't look out!'. He was clearly the worse for drink at the time.*

Again, Charles Matthews was allowed to cross-examine the witness:

Constable Butler, why did you not mention this threat to Constable Bishop before?

I did not attach any importance to the prisoner's threats, sir. Things of this sort are a very common occurrence.

Then perhaps, constable, we, in this court, should not attach any importance to it either?

The judge noticeably glared at the defence barrister, but Charles Matthews had made his point admirably. Further friction followed between the judge and the defence counsel, when the final prosecution witness was called.

John House had been in the Drax Arms around 9pm on the night PC Bishop had been killed. He was asked by the Crown to explain exactly what he saw:

I saw Henry Lock standing in the passage. Then Bishop came in there. Lock had a pint of beer in a pewter pot in one hand and a glass of beer in the other. Bishop took the glass of beer from Lock and drank it. Then he handed the glass back to Lock. As far as I could see, they were perfectly good friends.

This version of events appeared to contradict the prosecution counsel's case, and Charles Matthews quickly leapt on this anomaly during his cross-examination:

This seems extraordinary, that Constable Bishop actually went into the passageway of the public house.

Mr Batten, the prosecution barrister, interrupted, before the witness could answer, *Bishop went in there to see that all was quiet. That is all.*

Charles Matthews ignored the Crown's barrister and continued questioning John House,

And did Bishop and the other policeman come up behind Lock as he walked out of the Drax Arms?

Yes, replied John House, *Bishop put his hand on Lock's left shoulder and pushed him in the gate to Wennel's Yard. Lock was rather hard of hearing.*

So, in fact, Lock may not have heard the policeman ordering him to go home?, enquired Matthews.

No, sir. He was deaf.

Mr Justice Lopes once again interrupted the defence's cross-examination, *Mr Matthews, you will have ample time to question this witness fully during your defence.*

Thank you, your honour, but I shall be calling no witnesses!

Charles Matthews had developed a highly successful tactic of only questioning witnesses, in the middle of the prosecution's case, during his right of cross-examination. He felt that this both stole the Crown's thunder and enabled him to catch the witnesses off guard. This also gave him a greater opportunity, which he relished, of delivering a lengthy and verbose closing final submission to the jury.

He would not disappoint in this case. However, before the defence could begin, Dr Francis Lys was asked to provide details of his post-mortem examination to the court:

On the direction of the coroner, and in conjunction with Dr Daniel of Wareham, we made a post-mortem examination of the deceased on 21ª day of September. We found both his eyes black from blows, a blow on each temple, one on the nose, also blows on the left cheek, on the back of the hand, and the right elbow. There was also a small wound of the lower lip, and, on lifting the head, we found a jagged torn wound, about two inches long, just behind and above the left ear. On raising the scalp, a quantity of blood was found between the scalp and the bone, extending over the whole left side of the head. On opening up the head, a large quantity of clotted blood was found, which covered the whole left of the brain.

We then removed the brain, and noticed a fracture of the skull, on the left side, opposite and above the ear. The commencement of the fracture corresponded with the wound to the scalp. A vein also appeared to have burst at the back of the right eye.

No depressed bone could be found. The fracture was a long one, extending nearly four inches. The rest of the body was examined and appeared otherwise healthy.

Thank you Doctor, said Mr Justice Lopes, *Are you able to state a cause of death?*

In my opinion great violence must have been used to cause such an extensive fracture, and I think that the stone produced here in court would have been likely to produce the same. I am of the opinion that the cause of death was compression of the brain, due to the outpouring of blood, from vessels lacerated by the fracture.

After a recess for lunch, which may not have been as palatable as usual, following the graphic nature of the post-mortem evidence, Mr Justice Lopes invited Charles Matthews to begin the case for the defence.

Henry Lock's full trial would eventually last approximately five hours, of which the closing address by Charles

Matthews would take up fully one quarter of the entire proceedings. Whilst the public gallery seemed to enjoy his lengthy rhetoric, the patience of the judge was stretched to breaking point. In the era of quarterly Assizes, the courts were under pressure to process as many cases as possible in a relatively short interval. Trials seldom lasted longer than three hours, and juries rarely considered their verdicts for more than a few minutes. Victorian courtroom justice relied heavily on haste and expediency, rather than a methodically deliberated decision. In fact, the jury's room was rarely heated, nor were refreshments offered – a tactic that successfully helped to accelerate the decision process. No doubt, in the name of practicality, many innocent men and women were convicted; and many guilty defendants went free, with little or no right of appeal.

Although the Court of Appeal had been established in 1875 (thanks to a series of bills known as the *Judicature Acts 1873-1876*), the process was chaotic and unsatisfactory; and in reality, dealt mostly with civil cases. An appeal against a verdict in a murder trial was extremely rare and unlikely to succeed. In fact, a separate Court of Appeal, dealing solely with criminal cases, was not created until 1908. One all-encompassing Central Court of Appeal, involving a satisfactory appeals process, was not actually created until the passing of *Criminal Appeal Act 1966*. Even today, only about 3 per cent of appeals are ever successful.

In 1877, Charles Matthews clearly understood the importance of the counsel's closing address to the jury.

Charles Matthews confirmed that he would not be calling any witnesses on behalf of the defence, before turning and beginning his one-and-a-quarter-hour closing address to the Grand Jury (of which, this is a heavily edited version!):

Gentlemen of the jury, I address you on behalf of the prisoner. There can be no question, but that you are assembled here today for the purpose of discharging the most solemn, as well as the most painful, duty it could fall to a human being to discharge. You are here for the purpose of saying whether a fellow creature has committed an offence so grievous as murder that he can only atone for it, by the sacrifice of his life. But, when you take into consideration that the gift of life and the decree of death are in themselves functions appertaining to the divine ordinance of God, you must feel that you should approach your decision with every possible care, because, being mortal, you may be liable to error.

In saying these words, I do not dismiss the consequences of this dreadful situation. The consequences, it must be said, are not for you. I will let you view the facts as proved on the part of the Crown, and then say what is your verdict. A verdict that must meet both the ends of justice, mingled with the ends of mercy – for true justice cannot be done without true mercy.

Referring to the events of that evening, it is not unimportant to remember that the gateway leading into Wenell's Yard was closed, under normal circumstances, and the door secured by a latch. There was no disorder likely to produce a breach of the peace, although the men were singing a little louder than usual. Why did Constable Bishop choose to single out Henry Lock from the others? Yet, he did. Lock immediately obeyed him and walked towards his house. However, he was forced to the gate entering Wenell's Yard. But, being somewhat deaf, he had not properly heard Bishop's instructions. There was no resistance on the part of Lock, so, why should a hand, much less the hand of a policeman, be placed upon his shoulder? A struggle followed, and for what purpose, and with what authority, did the policeman draw his staff against an antagonist who had no such implement?

As to the words of the witnesses Arnold and Butler, who spoke of words previously spoken by the prisoner, you must remember that violent and excessive language, used under the influence of liquor, was one thing, and a threat is another. Words uttered when a man is under the influence of liquor are often forgotten in sobriety, and that is the end of it. In fact, both of the witnesses stated that these were ordinary expressions on Lock's part, and paid no attention to them.

But, to return to the incident, only when Lock was forced to his front door, forced into a scuffle, and violent hands had been laid upon him, did he retaliate. Smarting from the blow on the hand and the elbow, and smarting from the fact that an excessive instrument had been used against him, did he seize the first thing that came to hand and hurl it at the policeman.

If Lock had done what he did with express malice then the fact that he acted under provocation would not avail. But, can you really say that anything other than the heat of passion produced this tragic end?

I must also draw your attention to the possibility that the policeman's fracture may have been caused by the action of falling on the stones that surrounded the flower border, and not from the stone which struck him. You would be doing the prisoner an injustice if you did not consider this point.

Finally, in your solemn deliberations you will hear the voice of the prisoner himself, who will speak to you with a greater force than me.

At this point, Charles Matthews read out a preprepared statement written by Henry Lock. Prisoners were not encouraged to speak on their own behalf in court, as it was generally felt that they would prejudice their own case:

Gentlemen of the jury, these are the words of Henry Lock:

'I am very young. I am only twenty-two years old. It is true that in the heat of my tempestuous passion I have done that which my reason deplores, and which my conscience could never sanction. But I am very young, and all my life is before me in one sense; all my life is behind me in another. Of your mercy, of your impartiality, of your justice I crave. Not indeed my liberty, but my life'.

Thank you, members of the jury.

With that, Charles Matthews finally sat down, and Mr Justice Lopes reminded the jury that:

Murder was the killing of a person with malice aforethought, and that malice might be either expressed or implied. Manslaughter, on the other hand, was causing the death of another without malice but without legal justification. The question in this case, if you chose to find the prisoner guilty, is whether it is one of murder, or whether the circumstances reduced it to one of manslaughter. If you think it is a case of justifiable homicide, then the injury must have been inflicted immediately after the provocation.

But if, on the other hand, you think that Lock was actuated, not by provocation or passion of the moment, but by an old grudge, then it is murder.

The jury then retired to consider their verdict.

After a period of only ten minutes the jury returned. Asked if they had agreed on a verdict, the foreman replied, *Yes, your honour. We are all agreed that the prisoner is guilty of manslaughter.*

The black cloth cap, which was kept under the clerk's seat in the event of the death penalty being applied, would not be needed after all. Mr Justice Lopes thanked the jury, then turned to address the prisoner:

Henry Lock, the jury has taken a lenient view of the case, and although I do not say they are wrong, I cannot hide from my mind that your assault was committed under the most aggravated circumstances. I hope that you were not actuated by any feelings of malice, but I still cannot forget that, when the deceased was on the ground, your treatment of him was most brutal. It is, therefore, perfectly impossible that I pass upon you anything but the most severe sentence. The sentence of this court is that you shall be kept in penal servitude for ten years.

Henry Lock was immediately whisked away to the county jail in Dorchester, to begin his sentence.

Following his release, it does at least appear that Lock learned a very painful lesson. There are no further records of him re-offending.

The Dorset County Constabulary was originally formed in 1856. At the time of writing this story, eighteen officers have tragically died during the execution of their duty. Thomas Bishop was the first.

THE BRIDPORT BREAD RIOTS

What would she have done in the poverty now coming on me!

Thomas Hardy, *Far from the Madding Crowd*

The events of Monday April 29th, 1816, in Bridport may seem uncannily familiar to an audience today. When prices rise and well-paid employment is scarce, it is the poorest in society that are the most disproportionately affected. Yet, with no adequate recourse or audience for their grievances, the 'manufacturing poor' of Bridport were left with only one course of action in the spring of 1816 – to riot in desperation. The term 'manufacturing poor' was used by the establishment newspapers at the time, to refer to those who were employed, mostly in mills or in agriculture, and who, despite receiving a weekly wage, still had the 'audacity' to demand cheaper prices. In the days before trade unions, before the working man could expect to vote, and prior to the advent of the welfare state, there was little in the way of sympathy for the struggles of the poorest in society.

The end of the Napoleonic Wars with France had seen a return of peace and relative fortune to England.

The country had prospered in the one hundred years prior to 1815. Thanks to Britain's navy, empire, and trade routes, manufacturing employment grew substantially. As a consequence, while supply remained limited, agricultural prices increased markedly.

Despite wages for the working classes rising in Dorset during the eighteenth-century, these increases were insufficient to offset rising food inflation. Already low, living standards plummeted even further and many went hungry, particularly during the 1790s. Several poor summers followed, and the disastrous harvest of 1815 (often called 'the year without a summer', caused by the side-effect of the eruption of Mount Tambora in Indonesia) caused a worldwide reduction in crop yields and a resulting famine.

The market price of wheat rose to a record 113 shillings per quarter-hundredweight in 1800, whereas it had been only forty-eight shillings in 1760. In just five years between 1790 and 1795 the cost of living doubled. By 1800 it had doubled again. Meanwhile, more and more common land in Dorset was enclosed by farmers for the growing of food; however, this loss of public space robbed individuals of a place to keep livestock or grow their own food. To worsen matters for the hungry rural working classes, by the 1810s Dorset landowners were vigorously lobbying for harsher poaching laws and began to enforce the existing *Black Act* more stringently. Within a generation the *Night Poaching Act 1828* would eliminate the right for the poorer classes to remove or take any game, not only from open or enclosed land, but from any public road, path, or verge. With the exception of some small amendments in 1971, this act still remains in force today.

Meanwhile, the final straw came with the imposition of the *Corn Law* in 1815. This new legislation placed tariffs on imported cereal grain and was designed to protect domestic agricultural producers. The new laws prohibited the importation of corn until the price reached eighty shillings a bushel. This new restriction, coupled with the worldwide shortage, caused social unrest throughout rural England and in several large cities.

Matters finally reached boiling point in Bridport on 29th April when an angry mob of rioters targeted the town's millers and the bakers, who at that time had a reputation for greed and dishonesty. The estimate of the numbers taking part varied widely, and probably depended on the political agenda of the newspaper or local landowner reporting on the unrest. However, estimates varied from a few hundred to as many as two thousand.

Leading local residents, landowners, and magistrates were in no mood for this new-found spirit of rebellion among the Dorset working classes, as would later be recorded in the *Dorset County Chronicle*:

Last Monday morning, in consequence of the advance in the price of bread, several groups of the manufacturing poor assembled at different parts of Bridport, complaining of the grievance, added to their want of employ from the present stagnation of trade. Their numbers increasing, one of the most active bore a quartern (four-pound) *loaf through the streets on a pole: This drew together a great number of men, women, and children, who soon proceeded to acts of violence, demolishing the windows of the principal millers and bakers, and taking from the brewery of Messrs. Gundry three hogsheads of beer, which they drew in triumph to the centre of the town.*

The Riot Act was then read, but several hundred more having joined the mob, it was evident that nothing but the most prompt measures could prevent the dangerous consequences, likely to follow, and which were happily prevented by the exertions of some of the principal inhabitants, who rushed among the mob, destroyed the beer, seized the ringleaders, and in a very short time dispersed upwards of 2,000, committing the rioters to prison.

The *Riot Act 1714* had been introduced at a time of great civil disturbance in Britain; and gave local officials a mechanism to order the dispersal of 'any group of twelve people or more who were unlawfully, riotously, and tumultuously assembled together'. If the group failed to disperse within one hour, then 'anyone remaining gathered was guilty of a felony without benefit of clergy, punishable by death.'

By 1816 the *Riot Act* was being used more generally by the authorities to issue any stern warning or reprimand. The *Riot Act* fell into disuse by the 1970s and was eventually replaced by the *Public Order Act* in 1986 (as a consequence of the government's battle with striking miners in 1984-85), however, the term 'to read the Riot Act' to someone still lives on today, despite its original meaning being long forgotten.

Meanwhile, on the streets of Bridport, the reading of the *Act* had given the local magistrate the authority he required, and the rioting was eventually quashed, resulting in the arrest of several of the leading troublemakers, including the ringleader, John Toleman. The court case that followed gives us a unique insight into the attitude of the authorities to the grievances of those who dared to take on the British legal system.

The Summer Assizes at Dorchester, scheduled for Friday 2ⁿᵈ August 1816, gave the Crown the ideal opportunity to publicly present the rioters as both lawless and beneath contempt. The opinions of the presiding Judge, Mr Justice James Park KC, were only too obvious and were reported with relish by the establishment newspapers such as the *London Times*. Firmly an authority figure, Lord Park had been rumoured to be the illegitimate son of King George III. From the moment of his opening remarks to the Grand Jury, his sympathies became abundantly clear:

These assizes contain no cases, except one, which are not of ordinary occurrence. The case to which I allude is that of a great body of people having tumultuously assembled at Bridport, for very lawless and unjust purposes. It appears that this riot has been committed merely because these deluded persons imagined they should be able to redress certain grievances under which they laboured; but it was much to be lamented that they should think such a measure could add to their comforts. Unfortunately, if conviction should follow, they would find that the strong arm of the law must punish the wrongdoer: the magistrate does not bear the sword in vain, but must wield it for the purposes of virtue and justice. The grand jury would have to teach them this fearful lesson; so that when they retire to their private residences, it would be necessary to inform their less enlightened neighbours, that all attempts of this kind only increased the evil.

There is no occasion to plead poverty for the purposes of crime: charity was never withheld from the honest and industrious, but measures of this nature harden the hearts of the charitable.

Such persons are enemies to the good order and peace of society, and should be carefully avoided by the poor and illiterate.

Lord Park then alluded to the recent riots in other parts of the country, before praising the efforts of the police in suppressing the disturbances at Bridport.

The indictments were then read out by Mr Moore, on behalf of the Crown:

Jacob Powell, John Toleman the younger, Susannah Saunders, Hannah Powell, Samuel Follett, and Elizabeth Phillips, you are indicted for having unlawfully and riotously assembled, together with a great number of other evil-disposed persons, amounting to 200 and more, at Bridport, in the county of Dorset, on the 29th day of April last.

Prisoners at the bar, you stand indicted for an offence which, though not a felony, is almost as serious in its nature as any that could he brought before a jury. In consequence of the situation in which the country had been lately placed, a great clamour had been raised against the bakers of Bridport, and on the 29th of April a most serious and alarming riot took place in that town. It is fit that the labouring classes of the community should know, that by taking these steps they deprived themselves of the means of obtaining provisions, and thereby only increased the distresses of which they complained.

It is for the purpose of repressing this evil that the present prosecution had been instituted; and I shall call witnesses who will identify each of the prisoners as taking an active part in the riots. You attacked the bakers, and carried away great quantity of strong beer from the brewery of Messrs Gundry and Co, which you then intended to distribute among your deluded and lawless companions. In addition to these outrages, you placed loaves of bread on a pole, to instigate others to tumult, and used the most threatening language. If I should prove that all the prisoners here were implicated in these transactions, I feel sure that they will learn from the judge, that they have subjected themselves to the correction of the law.

The first witness, Mr Edward Nicholas, then described the
events of the 29th April for the court:

*Between one and three o'clock in the afternoon, I saw several hundred
persons assembled in the West Street; they had a brewer's dray with
several casks upon it, and were conducting themselves in a very riotous
and tumultuous manner. Five or six of them were seated upon the dray,
and the others surrounded it. They were chiefly men and carried staves
about a yard long. Jacob Powell was mounted on a cask in front of the
dray: he had a staff in his hand, and there was a loaf on the end of it;
it was held up so that the people might see it. I saw beer running out
of one of the casks.*

*This scene lasted nearly an hour, the noise was so great that I could
not hear any particular individual expression. Also, the town was
much disturbed, and the inhabitants were greatly alarmed. When
I heard that the Riot Act had been read, and that the mob did not
disperse, I offered, if ten would join me, to secure the ringleaders.*

*I advanced through the crowd towards the dray, and several men
followed me. I then secured Jacob Powell. Several windows in the
bakers' houses were broken, and the frames destroyed, but I could not
see who did it.*

The next witness, Richard Burden, a millwright, continued
the description of the afternoon's events:

*I live near Bridport, and I was there on the 29th April, and saw
several hundred persons assembled in West Street. They conducted
themselves very riotously for three or four hours. When M. Nicholas
proposed that we secure the ringleaders, I saw John Toleman near the
dray, and I helped to take him into custody, Toleman had a large stick
in his hand, with a loaf of bread on the top of it.*

Susannah Saunders was about two feet from the dray, but I did not see her do anything. A constable desired her to leave the dray, but she swore she would not leave it. She then attempted to strike Mr. Thomas Hounsel, one of the chief magistrates of the borough, who had got upon the dray to stave the casks, in order to prevent the mob from drinking the beer. She attempted to strike him with an umbrella, but I prevented her with my staff.

Jesse Cornick, a carpenter, was the next witness to testify for the prosecution:

The dray came up from South Street to West Street: it was then about two o'clock. I saw Hannah Powell near it, while I was assisting Mr Nicholas in securing the rioters. Hannah Powell then laid hold of a person I had in my custody, and tried to rescue him. I then also took her into custody.

William Dimond, one of Bridport's bakers, explained to the court how he was threatened by the rioters:

I saw Elizabeth Phillips at the head of the mob, when they were going to the brewery; she was about fifty yards before them. She came down the street very fast; there were three or four others with her. She said to me, 'Have you raised your bread?' I replied, 'I have not raised it.' She said, 'Damn you, we'll have your liver and lights out before night.'

Samuel Follett was accused of having broken the windows of the dwelling-house and shop of John Fowler the baker. Thomas Carter Galpin (the well-known portrait-painter and political satirist) who happened to be in Bridport on that day, was produced as a star witness, and he identified John Fowler as having committed this offence. Samuel Follett shook his head and denied the charge, but the privilege of cross-examination was not then available to the defendants at trial.

Defendants were at a strict disadvantage in court in the early years of the nineteenth-century. They were generally assumed to be guilty, and the trials proceeded on that basis. Judges and prosecutors (often the actual victim of the crime) dictated the proceedings and interpreted the law. Those accused were then expected to explain away the evidence against them, usually without

the benefit of legal counsel. Some improvements in this clear bias against those accused would eventually arrive during the tenure of Robert Peel as Home Secretary in 1822, and then following the introduction of the *Prisoners' Counsel Act* in 1836. However, in 1816, the defendants accused of rioting in Bridport could expect little in the way of a balanced or fair trial.

It was now the turn of the 'prisoners' (as defendants were referred to in court at that time). Jacob Powell stood nervously in court with his hands thrust into his pockets, and spoke directly to the grand jury:

I met the dray. A woman fell from it, and I went over to prevent the dray going over her. I stooped down to help, and then the people crowded about me, so I jumped on the dray, to escape being injured. Mr. Nicholas ordered me off, which I did not refuse. I was then ordered to go to the Town Hall, which I agreed to do. I had no staff in my hand.

John Toleman was next to defend himself: *I was standing in the street when the dray came up. Two women fell off, and I went to help one of them up. She had a loaf on a stick, and the next thing I knew, I was then taken into custody.*

Susannah Saunders testified: *I was not part of the mob till I was taken up by them. I had been at home at work.*

I was in the town, but did not break any windows, explained Hannah Powell.

Elizabeth Phillips, who held a baby in her arms throughout the trial, claimed that, *I was not part of it. I had been going up town to seek work.*

Despite having no formal legal experience, the group arranged for several associates to provide a sworn character reference, which was then read out in court:

We give each of the prisoners a good character. They have all been honest, industrious, sober, and peaceable, till the day of these transactions. Jacob Powell was a wool-comber; John Toleman, a flax-dresser. Susannah Saunders and Hannah Powell were spinsters; Elizabeth Phillips was the wife of a mason and has been much affected by these proceedings.

Mr Justice Park then addressed the members of the grand jury:

Members of the jury, the indictment against these prisoners is for having tumultuously assembled at Bridport, and making a riot to the disturbance of the King's peace; and certainly it appears that there was a very great riot on that day. This seems to have been occasioned by the high prices of provisions which then prevailed, and the rioters appeared to have seized the dray for the purpose, they supposed, of redressing some of their grievances. It was very unfortunate such a step should be taken, which could have no other effect than to increase the evil complained of. It is much to be lamented, that the prisoners, who appeared to be industrious persons, should have left their business to see what was going on. Taking their characters into consideration, if, you, the jury have any doubt of their having assisted in the riot, you should feel it your duty to acquit them; but if you are satisfied with the evidence, their former good conduct could not avail.

Mr Nicholas is entitled to great praise for his spirited conduct, and it was a very wise step on the part of the magistrates to save the beer. If that had not been done, the populace might have become intoxicated, which would have led to worse acts of mischief. In outrages of this nature, everyone is responsible for what the others did.

Jacob Powell has stated that he only tried to help a woman up: but how came he then among the people? He must have been there before the woman fell, even if his story is true. Mr Nicholas, however, has sworn that Jacob Powell was foremost on the dray. Toleman said he was standing in the street when the dray was brought up; but how came he to be there?

As to Susannah Saunders and Hannah Powell, it is much to be lamented that they, as honest industrious women, should have joined in such riotous measures.

Elizabeth Phillips does not appear to have acted with the mob and was fifty yards away; and though she made use of very violent expressions, she certainly took a less active part than the rest.

You, the jury must take these circumstances, and any former good character into consideration, when reaching your verdict.

The Jury then retired, but deliberated for only a few minutes, before returning a guilty verdict against all the prisoners.

At 5.30pm, Mr Justice Park passed sentence on the prisoners.

He first ordered that Jacob Powell, John Toleman the younger, Susannah Saunders, Hannah Powell, Elizabeth Phillips, and Samuel Follett, were brought up from the cells below:

Prisoners at the bar, you have been found guilty of a most outrageous riot at Bridport on the 29ᵗʰ of April last. It is fortunate for you that the magistrates took measures to suppress the disturbances immediately; for, if the mob had become infuriated with liquor, and any lives had been lost, you would all have been parties, and answerable for the consequences. Some of you, however, have been more active and forward than the rest. Your sentences would have been greater, if it had not been for the activity of the magistrates. But, taking all the circumstances of each case into consideration, I sentence Jacob Powell and Samuel Follett to be imprisoned for the space of twelve calendar months; John Toleman, to be imprisoned for nine months; Susannah Saunders and Hannah Powell to be imprisoned for six months; Elizabeth Phillips, who took a less active part, but used very violent expressions, to be imprisoned for three months. Take them away.

Strangely, in addition to their varying prison sentences, each of the prisoners was also fined one shilling (approximately £6 today).

The trial and subsequent punishments were widely publicised, leaving the working classes in Dorset in little doubt as to the establishment's attitude to such open displays of mutiny. The landowning classes in England had been hugely concerned that the embers of revolution, that had burned so brightly in France, would eventually drift across the channel and enflame the downtrodden agricultural poor of southern England. Anxious to stamp out any such flames of rebellion, the Bridport Bread Riots gave the establishment the perfect opportunity to make an example of those involved.

The harsh sentences appear to have succeeded in the short term. Meanwhile, living standards continued to erode among the poorer classes. It would be a further thirty years until the *Corn Law* was abolished.

In 1816, the prospect of obtaining a fair wage, a voice, and an acceptable standard of living seemed as distant as ever.

However, twenty-five miles away in the small village of Tolpuddle, a nineteen-year-old ploughman was preparing to take up the struggle...

UNDER THE SYCAMORE TREE

*The offhand decision of some commonplace mind high in office at
a critical moment influences the course of events for a hundred years.*

Thomas Hardy, *Life and Works*

Protests over high prices and lowering wages continued
among the poorer classes well into the 1820s and 1830s.
The *Enclosure Acts* reduced the rights of ordinary people
to the usage of common land, and there were continued
sporadic outbreaks of violence, with almost uninterrupted
unrest among agricultural workers across the south of
England. Embers from the French Revolution still fuelled
the frustration and resentment of downtrodden labourers
from Kent in the east, to Devon and Dorset in the west.
Hay ricks and barns were set alight in protests over low
wages and the government swept in new legislation to
deal with the growing insurrection. By 1830 more than
500 farm workers had been transported to the colonies for
'rioting, violence, rick burning and revolt.'

The paranoia of the landowning classes grew ever more
acute. In 1831, a seventeen-year-old was sentenced to
death at Worcester Assizes for setting a hayrick alight on his

employer's farm, and an eight-year-old boy was given two years' hard labour for the same offence. In 1833 a woman, Charlotte Long, was hanged at Gloucester Gaol for setting fire to three stacks of hay, despite having a new-born baby in her arms during her trial.

Measures to suppress the grievances of farm labourers were preventative as well as punitive. William Pitt's government had already taken repressive measures to control domestic unrest. The *Combination Acts* of 1799 and 1800 had banned 'unlawful combinations of workmen', and any 'collective bargaining' allowing workers to appeal for better working conditions or improvements in wages.

When the *Combination Acts* were repealed by Lord Liverpool's government in 1824, making Trade Unions no longer illegal, this seemed a step forward for workers. However, after an outbreak of strikes, restrictions were reintroduced in 1825, severely limiting Trade Union activities, even if not technically making them illegal. These new restrictions now left the actions of unions and their members open to the interpretation, rather than the letter, of the law.

Already mired in poverty, farm workers in the Dorset village of Tolpuddle were fully aware of the unrest spreading elsewhere in the country. Indeed, their community leader, the eloquent Methodist preacher George Loveless, had taken part in agricultural riots four years earlier. Despite this, and against the backdrop of the 'Swing Riots' and rising prices, the men protested peacefully when they first received the news that their pay would be cut from nine-shillings a week to seven-shillings (approximately £53 per week today) for a seventy-hour week. At that time, a typical agricultural labourer's rent and basic diet of bread, potatoes, tea, and basic essentials had already reached thirteen-shillings a week.

By 1832, the situation was desperate and a group of Tolpuddle workers, led by George Loveless, lobbied the landowners for a wage increase to ten-shillings per week. They asked the local vicar, the Rev Thomas Warren of St John's Church, to support them, pointing out that farm workers in the neighbouring counties of Wiltshire and Hampshire were already earning ten-shillings. The minister promised his support and the men requested that the Dorchester magistrates arbitrate in their dispute with the local landowners. Rev Warren agreed to act as witness to the agreement between the farm labourers and landowners; only to later deny that any such pact existed when the landowners reneged on the arrangement.

James Frampton, the Squire of Moreton and Dorset's leading magistrate, told the men that he had no power to fix wages and promptly threatened to reduce their pay to six-shillings per week for their presumption in asking. He also warned the men that any further agitation may lead to a further reduction in pay. Frampton feared the threat of organised labour to his family's wealth and land, and he was determined to stamp out any insurrection among the agricultural workers in the county.

To illustrate James Frampton's wealth at that time, it is worth noting that in 1832 his recorded rental income from the estates he owned, just in the villages surrounding Tolpuddle, amounted to over £6,800 (today's equivalent of £1 million). He also held other estates in Dorset and Devon. In marked contrast, the Tolpuddle labourers, earning just nine shillings a week, would have been required to work for seventy hours a week, fifty-two weeks a year, for almost three-hundred years to earn the equivalent sum.

In 1833, against this backdrop of obstruction, a group of Tolpuddle workers united to form a Friendly Society of Agricultural Labourers, determined to protect their rights, and to demand wages of no less than ten-shillings per week. The new society aligned itself with the recently created Grand National Consolidated 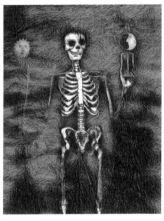 Trades Union in London, and by December of 1833 they were meeting regularly, either under the 150-year-old sycamore tree on the village green, or in the upper room of Thomas Standfield's cottage in the village. Entry into the society involved a payment of one shilling, and the swearing of an oath of secrecy, made with one hand resting on the Bible. This secret oath and initiation ceremony included a pledge not to reveal anything of the society's proceedings, the names of its members, or the dues they paid. The ritual aspect of the initiation, and its degree of seriousness, was emphasised at the climax, when the new member, as a symbol of the potential consequences for breaking his vow, was suddenly confronted with a life-size painting of a skeleton.

Meanwhile, news of the flourishing society reached James Frampton, who began to gather evidence against the organisation. The formation of a trade union was legal, of course; and there was little James Frampton could do to prevent the society from growing in strength. However, the local magistrate (probably acting on a tip-off) discovered that the society employed the use of a secret oath and ritual. If he could prove the existence of such a ceremony, there would be a basis to arrest the members under the *Unlawful Oaths Act* of 1797. On 9th December 1833, a labourer named Edward Legg attended a meeting of the society in Thomas Standfield's home. Legg would later act as the Crown's chief witness at the trial of the Tolpuddle men and had undoubtedly been planted among the union's membership by James Frampton.

Next, Frampton consulted Lord Melbourne, the Home Secretary, informing him that societies were now being formed among the agricultural labourers, which included the taking of clandestine vows and the swearing of secret oaths. It appears that Lord Melbourne, despite his brother-in-law being MP for Dorset, and a staunch ally of Frampton's, advised Frampton to exercise some caution and gather his evidence carefully, since no further action was taken for two months. Under the terms of the *Unlawful Oaths Act*, any person found guilty of taking an oath with the intention of 'engaging in any mutinous or seditious Purpose; or to disturb the public peace; or to be of any Association, Society, or Confederacy, formed for any such Purpose', could be transported to the colonies 'for any term not exceeding seven years.'

James Frampton devised a cunning and underhand plan to ensure that the conspirators were caught 'red-handed'.

He decided to publish and distribute a cautionary handbill which warned against the swearing of unlawful oaths. And so, on Saturday 22nd February 1834, the handbill was distributed in and around the village of Tolpuddle, reminding the public that 'mischievous and designing persons' had been organising union meetings, asking members to swear 'unlawful oaths'. The leaflet, in large letters, gave the unambiguous warning that anyone convicted would be 'Guilty of Felony'. The trap was now set.

Two days later, on the morning of Monday 24th February, George Loveless set off for work. He said goodbye to his wife of ten years, Betsy, and their three children and, along with the other farm workers in Tolpuddle, started out on his dreary and chilly trudge to work in the dim light of a February morning. As they did so, thirty-seven-year-old Loveless was served with an arrest warrant. Loveless, along with five fellow farm labourers, were charged with swearing an illegal oath.

George Loveless, his brother James, Thomas Standfield (who had been a witness at George's wedding a decade earlier), John Standfield (Thomas's son), James Hammett, and James Brine, were arrested and forced to march in their heavy boots and working smocks the ten-mile journey along the Dorchester Road to Wollaston House in Durngate Street, the home of Magistrate Charlton Byam Wollaston (who was also James Frampton's half-brother). Ironically, the six men would have been taken along the road on which the museum built in their honour now stands.

Waiting at the large and imposing Georgian house with
CB Wollaston was James Frampton. Together, they swiftly
questioned and identified the six men as being present
and taking part in a trade union meeting on 9th December
1833, in Tolpuddle. The men were immediately committed
to Dorchester County Gaol, where they were stripped,
searched and shaven bald, before being locked up to await
trial. When the prison guards searched George Loveless,
one of the infamous handbills, warning against the
swearing of unlawful oaths, was discovered in his pocket.

Whilst awaiting trial in a damp and cold prison cell, which
worsened the health of George Loveless considerably, he
famously scribbled these words from the union hymn, *The
Gathering of the Unions* on a scrap of paper:

> *God is our guide! from field, from wave,*
> *From plough, from anvil, and from loom;*
> *We come, our country's rights to save,*
> *And speak a tyrant faction's doom:*
> *We raise the watch-word liberty;*
> *We will, we will, we will be free.*

These few words have become forever associated with
George Loveless but were in fact originally composed by
Harriet Martineau and Eliza Flower, and were sung two
years earlier in May 1832, by over 100,000 workers at a
pre-Reform Bill meeting in Birmingham known as The
Gathering of the Political Unions. Perhaps George Loveless
even attended the meeting, although it is unlikely that he
would have been given leave to travel so far.

Nineteen days later, on 15th March 1834, the six men were transferred to the spartan cell block underneath the County Court to await trial. Finally, after in a week in the windowless cell, the pomp and ceremony of the Lent Assizes began, and the gentlemen of the grand jury were sworn in. In an age before juries were selected from a balanced cross-section of society, the grand jury in the case of the Tolpuddle Martyrs comprised of local magistrates including CB Wollaston and James Frampton (who had been involved in both the arrest and questioning of the six men, and were well known anti-reformers), and the splendidly named Thomas Horlock Bastard, Henry Bankes, the Tory MP and opponent of reform, and several landowning farmers and squires, who all opposed wage increases for agricultural workers.

The six men were led up narrow wooden steps and took their place in the cramped dock while the evidence against them was read out. Edward Legg, and others, explained the ritual behind the oath swearing:

James Loveless and George Loveless asked if we were ready to have our eyes blindfolded; we said yes. We then bound our handkerchiefs round our eyes; we were then led through a passage into another room on the same floor. On getting into that room a paper was read to us, I think it came from the Bible. We then got up, turned ourselves around, and took the covering from our eyes. A light was in the room. Something, a picture I think, which had the appearance of a skeleton, was shown to us. James Loveless then said, 'Remember your end'.

I did not know the exact meaning of the rules, something was said about paying a shilling on entering the Society, and a penny a week afterwards to support the men who were out of work – meaning those

*who had struck, till their masters should raise their wages. I know the
meaning of the word 'strike', but I don't recollect that I heard the word
used that night.*

In truth, the outcome of the trial never looked in doubt.
Even the eloquence of George Loveless (who requested the
opportunity to speak in court) could not rescue the men's
fate:

My Lord, he pleaded, *if we have violated any law, it was not done
intentionally. We have injured no man's reputation, character, person,
or property. We were uniting together to preserve ourselves, our wives
and our children from utter degradation and starvation, We challenge
any man, or number of men, to prove that we have acted, or intended
to act, different from the above statement.*

Sadly, his words fell on deaf ears. After a two-day trial,
the six men were sentenced by the grand jury to seven
years' transportation to New South Wales, Australia - the
maximum sentence available under the *Unlawful Oaths Act.*
The judge, Baron Williams, made his opinion in the case
abundantly clear, stating that the safety of the country was
at stake:

It is for the sake of example, and *on which the security of the country
and the maintenance of the law upon which it depends, makes it
indispensable to pass the sentence the law has pointed out. I feel I have
no discretion in a case of this sort, and accordingly the sentence is that
each of you be transported for seven years.*

The men were taken away to be prepared for
transportation to Botany Bay in New South Wales,
Australia. On 11th April, James Loveless, Thomas and
John Standfield, James Hammett, and James Brine were

shackled aboard the prison hulk *Surry* to begin their arduous 13,000-miles journey.

After arriving on 17ᵗʰ August, the men were quickly assigned as farm labourers. George Loveless, however, had been too ill to be transported with his comrades and sailed six weeks later from Portsmouth, bound for Van Diemen's Land (now Tasmania) aboard the transport ship *William Metcalf*. Loveless endured inhuman conditions at sea which he would later detail:

I shared a dormitory with 240 men, shut down together and locked in a prison, the greater part of them such monsters as I never expect to see and whose conduct I am not capable of describing.

A small bed, pillow and blanket was allowed for each man, which would have contributed greatly to our comfort had there been room sufficient to have lain on them, but we could not. A berth about five feet six inches was all that was allowed for six men to occupy day and night, with the exception of four hours we were allowed daily on deck, two hours in the forenoon, and two in the afternoon. For nearly ten weeks out of fourteen on board, I was not able to lie down at length to take rest.

George Loveless would also later recall his experiences in Van Diemen's Land in his publication, *Victims of Whiggery*:

In fine weather, we could lie in bed and view the stars, in foul weather, feel the wind and rain; and this added more than a little to increase those rheumatic pains which were first brought on by cold irons round the legs and the hard laying, and which in all probability, will be my companion until I reach the tomb.

The others suffered hardships too. Thomas Standfield, the oldest of the six men, became a shepherd and was given a small hut, six feet high and eighteen inches wide in which to shelter. He was forced to walk four miles each night to collect his rations.

James Brine was sent to a farm on the Hunter River. He was given one-shilling and a small blanket and told to walk until he found the farm. He was robbed on the way and when he finally reached the farm, his employer forced him to dig post holes for six months, gave him no fresh bedding, leaving him no choice but to sleep on the bare ground.

Meanwhile, in England, public outcry at the harsh sentences spread rapidly. The Tolpuddle men soon became 'martyrs' for the cause of trade unionism, as anger at their severe punishment grew. In April 1834 a huge protest march took place in London. The Home Office was forced to enrol 5,000 special constables to maintain order. Petitions were presented to parliament containing an estimated 800,000 signatures. The London Central Dorchester Committee was formed to raise funds, print pamphlets, and increase public support for the cause. Meanwhile, Welsh philanthropist, Robert Owen, and reformer, William Cobbett, kept relentless pressure on the government.

Finally, in March 1836, the government, in the form of new home secretary, Lord John Russell, were forced to rescind the sentences of the six men. Initially, there was some confusion and delay as the men were only offered unsatisfactory conditional pardons. However, eventually, all six men received a full and free pardon. Arrangements were then made for their return. George Loveless docked in England on 13th June 1837. James Loveless, Thomas and John Standfield, together with James Brine, arrived in Plymouth on 17ᵗʰ March 1838 to a rapturous welcome. James Hammett's return was delayed after he received an eighteen-month sentence for assault in Australia. He finally arrived back in England during August 1839.

Unsurprisingly, five of the men chose not to remain in Tolpuddle and eventually emigrated to London in Upper Canada (now Ontario), where they lived out the rest of their lives.

James Hammett was the only one of the Tolpuddle Martyrs who remained in the village. He passed away in the Dorchester Workhouse in 1891 at the age of 79 and is buried in the churchyard of St John's in Tolpuddle.

The village of Tolpuddle has since become an important landmark in the history of the trade union movement in Britain. In 1934, to mark the centenary of the Tolpuddle Martyrs' transportation, the Trade Union Congress built the Memorial Cottages, in which the Martyrs' Museum is now housed. There are also other celebrations of the men's story which can still be viewed in the village, including the remains of the approximately 330-year-old sycamore tree, under which their early meetings were held, the old chapel, and Thomas Standfield's cottage. There is also an annual festival to honour the memory of the Martyrs.

In Dorchester too, there are reminders of the men's courage and sacrifice. The old courthouse and cells in the Shire Hall are now a museum, and a poignant reminder of the men's suffering and sacrifice.

In an ironic twist of fate, Wollaston House in Durngate Street, the former home of CB Wollaston, the magistrate's home to which the six men were first taken, has become the headquarters of the Dorset County Show, the annual showpiece for farmers, agriculture, and rural life in the county.

The two 'villains' of the piece, CB Wollaston and James Frampton, lived out their lives in relative prosperity, Wollaston remained a highly respected barrister and Official Recorder of Dorchester. He translated *The Satires of Persius* from their original Greek and his portrait hangs in the National Portrait Gallery. He died two years after the Martyrs had returned to England and is buried at St Nicholas' Church in Moreton, alongside James Frampton and TE Lawrence ('Lawrence of Arabia').

There has been some attempt in recent years to add some perspective to the role of James Frampton in the affair of the Tolpuddle Martyrs. After all, although he was responsible for bringing the six men to trial, it was not actually he who passed the harshest possible sentence on the men. In fact, in Dorset, only twelve men were ever transported to Australia.

No doubt a product of his time, the wealthy Frampton was expected to fulfil the role of High Sheriff of Dorset at the age of only twenty-four. Like the majority of his contemporaries he believed that the class structure was the pre-ordained way of things; and that the poorer classes should 'know their place'. Frampton had looked in horror at the bloodshed of the French Revolution and the growing agitation at home. Horrified by the threat of revolution and violence during the 'Swing Riots', he had previously ordered the boarding up of the ground floor windows and doors at his Moreton House estate, and even led a mounted patrol of the Dorset Yeomanry to dissuade any troublemakers. He clearly had little sympathy for the struggles of the agricultural labourers in the county.

However, perhaps the most damning piece of evidence against James Frampton is the less well-known case of the Milton Abbas Martyrs. In 1803, while still a young magistrate, Frampton sentenced six agricultural labourers from the Dorset village of Milton Abbas to two months hard labour at Dorchester Gaol for conspiring with others to increase their wages. Perhaps, had these six men's punishment been harsher, they might also be as well remembered and revered.

Finally, the role of the London Central Dorchester Committee should not be forgotten. Formed in August 1834, following the Tolpuddle men's transportation to Australia, the Committee became a focal point for the national pressure placed on the government, as well as providing profound financial support for the families of the six men. The Committee's balance sheet for the period 1835-1839 shows that they received £71 in income from the sale of *Victims of Whiggery*, by George Loveless, yet advanced £349 19s 1d in financial support to the families of the six men – more than £50,000 today.

THE JEALOUS HUSBAND
(PART ONE)

There is a condition worse than blindness,
and that is seeing something that is not there.

Thomas Hardy, Tess of the D'Urbervilles

Unusually, on Friday 6th June 1902, the Dorset Assizes at
Dorchester saw not one, but two, murder trials take place.
Although the time was now fast approaching 8pm, the
judge, Mr Thomas Bucknill, wanted the second case of
murder completed before the weekend. He informed the
court that he was required in Wells by Monday morning
to begin the Somerset Assizes and had no intention of
working over the weekend!

Thomas Bucknill, a prominent Freemason and former
Conservative Member of Parliament, would later become
celebrated as the judge who sentenced the poisoner
Frederick Seddon to death in 1912, in one of the twentieth-
century's most notorious murder trials. After being
convicted, Seddon famously appealed directly to Thomas
Bucknill, as a brother Freemason:

In the name of the Great Architect of the Universe, overturn the
verdict.

Bucknill was reported as saying, as he fought back his emotions:

We both belong to the same brotherhood, and though that can have no influence with me, this is painful beyond words to have to say what I am saying. Our brotherhood does not encourage crime, it condemns it.

Returning to the events of June 1902, Mr Justice Bucknill was about to face a very different type of prisoner to his future adversary, the tall, polished, and confident Frederick Seddon.

The unruly public gallery of the courtroom had been cleared to allow the charge against Frank Burden to be read aloud by the Clerk of the Assizes:

Prisoner at the bar, the charge against you is that on February 11ᵗʰ you feloniously, wilfully, and of malice aforethought, did kill Emily Burden. How do you plead?'

Frank Burden, described as 'undersized, but thick set, with un-shapely features, a sallow face, and large eyes,' scanned the court with an expression of mingled curiosity and anxiety, before answering in a clear voice, 'Not guilty.'

Mr Justice Bucknill then announced, 'The public can now be re-admitted, and I hope they will behave themselves.'

The story of Frank Burden and his young wife Emily really begins three years earlier when the couple married in April of 1899. Frank, the eldest of three brothers, and Emily both came from Semley, near Tisbury, in Wiltshire, and moved to the Isle of Portland two days after their wedding when Frank took a gardening job for a landowning gentleman there named Edward Pierce.

To the outside world, Frank and Emily seemed a
mismatched couple. Frank was small, physically
unattractive, and 'un-shapely'. Due to a spinal deformity,
he walked with a stooped back, making him appear
even shorter. Although hardworking and sober, he was
not particularly intelligent. In contrast, Emily was well
educated, having been the school mistress at Semley.
She was tall, elegant, shapely, and beautiful, as well as,
at twenty-two years old, being almost a decade younger
than her new husband. Nevertheless, the couple seemed
genuinely happy. In April 1900, the ambitious Frank rented
part of a double-fronted tenement at No. 95, in the hamlet
of Reforne, from a Mrs Cook of Weymouth. The area
now forms part of Easton and, shortly after the murder of
Emily Burden, No. 95 was demolished and replaced with a
more modern house.

The newly married couple occupied one half of the
building, which comprised a dwelling room on the ground
floor, a bedroom above, and an attic-room. The other half
of the property was firstly lived in by the Scard family, and
later by Mr and Mrs Damon. Frank Burden soon decided
to offer the attic room to a lodger, to help cover the rent.
John (Jack) Roberts moved in during November 1900; and
stayed until January 1902. Frank's younger brother, Ernest,
also took lodgings in the attic room in August 1901, and
remained there until Emily's death.

Frank worked hard, and the couple appeared to be
outwardly respectable. He took a second job as a labourer
at a local sawmill, meaning he was away from home
for many hours. However, two shadows seem to have
simultaneously cast a veil over their relationship. Firstly,
Frank believed that his spinal deformity meant that he was

unable to father a child, although, there does not appear
to be any medical evidence of this. Frank did not inform
Emily of his fears, although he did tell his brother Ernest.
He swore his brother to secrecy; promising to tell Emily
only when the time was right.

It also seems that there was a certain amount of gossip in
the community regarding the living arrangements at No. 95
Reforne. Local innuendo suggested that Emily was involved
in an affair with the lodger John Roberts. Inevitably these
rumours reached Frank Burden; primarily from an elderly
lady named Alice Flew. She informed Burden that his wife
and the lodger John Roberts 'were very much together'
and that she had seen them 'play draughts together.'
Despite hearing these rumours, however, Burden does not
appear to have acted on them until November 1901. It
was during that month that Emily informed Frank that she
was expecting a baby. His reaction took her completely by
surprise.

'What man have you been with?', he demanded to know.

She denied the accusation. However, from that moment
he became continually suspicious and intently jealous.
Although he did not directly confront John Roberts, he
gave the lodger notice to be out of the house by 4th January,
claiming that he now needed the space in the attic room.

Throughout that night the argument continued. Frank
threatened to place a ladder against the bedroom window
and return home unexpectedly to catch her with her
lover. The couple's struggle became a physical one with
Frank inflicting a prolonged assault on his wife, although
the injuries and bruises she received were covered by

her clothing. The following day their neighbour, Mrs Alice Scard, witnessed the bruising on Emily's legs and attempted to mediate the couple's differences. Emily then wrote to her mother, Caroline Green, begging for enough money to allow her to leave her husband. This, in turn, prompted a visit from Emily's mother on 18th January 1902, during which time she gave Emily a gold sovereign to assist her in returning home to Wiltshire. On her arrival at her daughter's house, Caroline Green found Frank unable to sleep, complaining of an intense pain in his head.

Thanks to some mediation from Emily's mother and the neighbour Alice Scard, it appears that the couple then made some effort to save their relationship.

With the lodger now departed, Frank wrote to Emily's mother on 31st January and expressed his sorrow at the way he had treated their daughter.

95, Reforne. 31st January 1902

Dear Mother and Father,

I suppose you will be surprised to hear from me. I am writing to tell you that we settled everything all right, before we had your letter. Therefore, I promised Em that I would go on better, be the same to her as I used to be - whatever may come, let it share the same as us – therefore you both can rest your hearts, contented that she shan't want for anything. I am very sorry that it happened, but never mind, it shall be better for the future. Mrs Scard begs us not to part, as we have it comfortable. I suppose neither of us would be anything parted – those are Em's own words.

But never mind, I will be as good to her as I can. Em said she will feel better satisfied, as I promised her in front of Mrs Scard to go on better. Neither of us want to part as we have love for one another. We both agreed if everything go all right (with the birth of the baby), *when 'tis over, Em shall come up to you for a time.*

I suppose Em told you all about the blows. Em struck me first in the face, made my nose bleed all over the bedclothes. And in temper I struck her again, but she is better now. Now I must close.

Kind love to you all,

From

Frank

Evidently, from his use of the phrase 'whatever may come' and 'it', Frank still maintained his belief that he was not the father of Emily's baby. Although his letter shows some contrition and remorse, and even a promise to treat the unborn child as his own, Frank again argued with his wife on the same day as the letter was posted to Wiltshire. In a disagreement witnessed by the neighbour, Frank Burden said to Emily, 'Where are you going to, gal, dressed like that?'

Emily showed him the gold sovereign from her mother and answered, 'I'm going home.'

'I'll see about that.' Frank replied furiously. He turned and told the neighbour Mrs Scard accusingly, 'I have no doubt you knew she was transgressing. Look what she's got here.' He pointed to the gold sovereign.

His remorseful letter provoked the following response from Emily's mother:

High-Street, Hindon, 2nd February, 1902

My dear Frank,

Very glad I was to hear from you. God only knows what it has been to me. I do hope with all my heart that you will never say such dreadful things to her again. I know that my dear child is very free to talk, but I know that there is no harm in what she says. She lets little things slip from her without a thought. Then there is harm made of it, but no one on the face of the earth will ever make me think she has been unfaithful to you.

She always had too much love for you to do such a thing, and I do hope you will never be led away by others to think such a thing of her. I know her dear heart has almost broken with the trouble she had, but I do trust that it will never occur again. I should be very sorry for you to be parted. It would be very bad for two young people, all for the sake of a dear child coming into the world.

You ought to be pleased. She has been so long free, and, my dear Frank, I do hope you will be kind to her. I have had nine children, but, thank God, my husband was always kind to me. I do hope you will let her have the money to manage, for I know she doesn't waste your money, and there will be many little things she has to get ready.

I do pray then, Frank, that you will both be happy, the same as before, and I do hope that everything unpleasant will never be brought up again, or she must come home. It all seems so cruel.

Now, dear Frank, give my love to my dear child. I hope you will both make up for all, and be very happy. Tell my dear child I will write to-morrow,

With my love to you,
From Mother

Sadly, this genuinely affectionate and forgiving letter from Emily's mother did little to allay Frank's suspicious and jealous nature. Even with Roberts the lodger gone, matters only worsened. Frank Burden now became convinced that Emily was having extra-marital affairs with two other men - Jack Pearce, the rent collector, and Abraham Winter, a monumental stonemason (who had previously worked with her husband at the sawmill).

The following conversation then took place between Burden and Jack Pearce:

Burden: *You have been there for the rent in the summer dozens of times when I have been in the garden.*

Pearce: *Either winter or summer, you were present nine times out of ten.*

Burden: *On Saturday week, you took ten shillings from my wife for rent. Another man then told me that 'Gipsy Pearce's son had been up to my house with my wife and that a hard-working little fellow like me ought to know it'.*

Pearce: *I went to the house, and I saw that your wife had been crying. We only spoke about the drainage.*

Burden: *Oh, so you have been up here?*

Pearce: *That is my business. But if you want to know, I have not been in the house.*

Burden: *False, false!*

Frank Burden also challenged Abraham Winter, to whom he had first introduced his wife at the Parish Festival. He accused Winter of chasing after Emily in the street and of 'using language to her that makes me ashamed of you'.

Frank's brother, Ernest, was forced to confront him and make Frank promise not to quarrel with Emily, nor inflict any further harm on her.

Matters reached a head on Tuesday 11th February. Frank returned from work at 5pm and sat down to eat with Emily and Ernest. All seemed peaceful for a brief moment, until Frank suddenly complained about the fish he had been served for his tea, *This is not our day for fish! You don't care about the house now. You care about those men most. You don't care about me.*

Ernest, embarrassed and worried for his sister-in-law, was forced to intervene, *It was a very good tea, you should not bother about having fish, Frank.*

Frank's brother needed to return to work shortly and was obviously worried about Emily's wellbeing. He refused to leave the house unless Frank promised to stop quarrelling with Emily. Frank, seeming to calm down, did agree to this and Ernest duly left the house, leaving Emily and her husband alone. From the moment Ernest shut the front door, Frank's temper returned. Meanwhile, in the other half of the house, the new neighbour, Mrs Ellen Damon, was also alone and could not help overhearing the argument:

Someone has been up here twice a week, oftener than he used to come, Frank spat out accusingly, *Some other man told me so.*

Tell me who the man is! Emily retorted.

I will not!

Emily responded, *It is only you has wicked thoughts. If that's what you think, I will go at once. I am leaving.*

She then ran upstairs, presumably to begin packing. Frank locked the front door and calmly followed her upstairs.

Next door, Mrs Damon heard the sound of footsteps on the stairwell, followed by a commotion and a single piercing scream emanating from the Burden's bedroom. She jumped up and rushed to her neighbour's front door but could not gain entry. In a panic, Mrs Damon ran to the neighbouring house (No. 93) and pleaded with the owner Mr Jonathan Lano, a local magistrate, to help. He refused, despite Mrs Damon's appeal, not wishing to become involved in a domestic affair. Worried for Emily's wellbeing, Mrs Damon returned to No. 95. As she passed through the front door, she noticed the silhouetted shadow of Frank Burden on the window. She knew he was still in the house. From the internal passageway Mrs Damon heard the distinctive sound of the bolt on the back door being pulled back. Bravely, she ran back out of the front door and around the side of the house into the small backyard. As she did so, Frank Burden pushed past her and made his escape over the wall and through the other gardens. Mrs Damon screamed and cried out, 'You brute! You brute!'

Mrs Damon then returned inside No. 95 from the small yard and nervously called up the shadowy stairwell, 'Missus? Missus Emily?' Receiving no response, she took a candle and made her way up the narrow staircase and into the Burden's bedroom. Emily's unmoving body lay on the floor, soaked in blood, with numerous wounds to her stomach, hands, and throat.

By this time, alerted by the commotion, the next-door neighbour, Mr Lano, accompanied by his two sons, Reginald and Richard, burst into the room. On seeing the horror that confronted him, he took charge. Returning to his house, Mr Lano telephoned a friend and asked him to go and fetch the police at once, the police station on Portland having no telephone line of its own in 1902.

The doctor was also called, but he was unable to assist Emily, who had already passed away from severe blood loss.

In the meantime, Frank Burden hastily made his escape. Quickly making his way south, he spent the night sleeping rough in the grounds of Pennsylvania Castle. From there, he appears to have wandered aimlessly, eventually making his way to a secluded point at Church Ope Cove where he apparently attempted to drown himself. During this time, news of the horrific murder spread across Portland.

By dawn, every policeman and working man, making his way to work, was on the lookout for Frank Burden.

Forty minutes before sunrise, in the early morning twilight, he was spotted near to Wakeham railway bridge by a quarryman, William Butts Elliot, who was on his way to work. The wet, cold, and shivering Burden was immediately recognised by Elliot, who placed his hand on Burden's shoulder and said, 'Ha, you are just the bloke that everyone is looking for!'

Elliot, with assistance from two other men, handed Burden over to the police. Burden offered no resistance. As he was restrained by PC Osman, Burden asked, 'Is she dead?'

'Yes.' replied the policeman, 'you'll see that in another day, when you get a rope around your neck'. Burdon replied:

She was not dead when I left her. This is all through men going to my house when I am away. We had words about it, and this is all through my temper. Jack Pearce and Abraham Winter both stayed about there when I was away. I tried to drown myself but could not. I jumped in three times.

Burden was now in police custody. An enquiry into the events of the previous night could begin.

THE JEALOUS HUSBAND
(PART TWO)

People go on marrying because they can't resist natural forces, although many of them may know perfectly well that they are possibly buying a month's pleasure with a life's discomfort.

Thomas Hardy, *Jude the Obscure*

Frank Burden was charged with Emily's murder and placed in the cells. This gave the police time to search the crime scene at No. 95 Reforne and begin their enquiries.

An initial search of the upstairs bedroom was made by Constable Arnold. On the far side of the bed from where Emily's body had been found, carefully pushed between the mattress and the bed frame, Constable Arnold discovered a cut-throat razor and blood soaked, brown buckhorn-handled pocket-knife, with a three-inch blade. The blades of both weapons had been carefully closed inside their respective handles. An attempt had clearly been made to hide the items. At the police station, Frank Burden's wet clothing was removed, and an examination made. However, it was noted that his jacket and cap were dry, indicating that he must have removed them before entering the water. What appeared to be bloodstains were also found on his trousers and shirt. In addition, a pencil, together with three partly written letters were found stuffed into the pockets. The unfinished letters appeared to indicate that Frank Burden had endeavoured to construct either a suicide note, or a confession of sorts, or perhaps both. It seems he had not been able to finish any of his three rambling and disjointed attempts:

Dear Father and Mother,
I am so… to tell you I have killed Em, all through December. Jack Pearce – landlord and Ab Winter, the monumental mason told me.

And again, on another piece of paper,

Dear Father and Mother,
My brains are upside down. Ab. Winter…

Finally, Frank's last attempt was scrawled across the previous note,

Was Jack Pearce and Ab. She told me her own self it was Ab. Winter and Jack Pearce.

Two days after Emily's murder, Frank was allowed to write to his parents from his cell at the police station:

Police-station, Portland, Dorset, Feb. 13th

My dear Mother and Father,

Just a line to tell you what I have done. I suppose you will feel it very much. Hope Walter and Ernest will come and see me when they come back. I hope they will, for I want to have a word with them. She drove me to kill her. She would not stop. Her games nearly drove me out of

my mind. I was nearly crazy when I done it. I own up to it. I could not help myself. She was a bad one to drive me to do it.

I hope and trust God will forgive what I have done. Dear Mother, don't worry about me, for I am not worth it now. I will pray to God for all the time I am in this world. I suppose everybody will cry shame at me. If they do, I can't help it. All her fault. She drove me to do it. I hope and trust you won't make yourself bad over it. I wish I never seen her. Too late now. Dear Mother, if I never see you again, I hope and trust I may see you again in Heaven, for I am going to pray with all my heart for forgiveness. I hope I shall get it, but I'm afraid I shan't.

Give my love to all. I don't know how soon it will come. The sooner the better, for I am tired of this life. I hope Father will bear up if he can.

From your ever true and loving son,

Frank

Sadly, Frank's father, Alfred, did not 'bear up if he can', as his son had hoped. He never recovered from the shock and shame of his son's actions and died four years later at the age of sixty-four.

Meanwhile, Frank Burden was scheduled to be taken by train to Weymouth to face an initial magistrates' hearing at Weymouth Police Court. A rumour spread that the prisoner would leave Portland on the 9.32am train to Weymouth, and a large throng gathered, all anxious to see the man accused of Emily's murder. However, the police had no intention of allowing the crowd's morbid fascination to be satisfied, and arranged for a horse-and-

trap to pull up behind the police station instead. Burden
was then secretly whisked away to the magistrates' court
in Weymouth. The large crowd gathered at the station did
not seem unduly disappointed; they simply boarded the
9.32 train *en masse* and travelled to the magistrates' hearing
instead!

Another statement made by Frank to Sergeant Northover,
during his incarceration at the Portland police station, was
read out at the magistrates' hearing. This new version of
the events on 11ᵗʰ February seemed to differ somewhat
from the evidence of the neighbour, Mrs Damon, and from
Frank's earlier confession. According to his new statement,
Frank testified that:

*We had some words at teatime. She went upstairs and took off some of
her clothes to mend, her corsets. I went up after her. I said,*

'Now, girl, what is it to be? Let's die together.'

*I took the razor, and she then said, 'Don't kill me, Frank, kiss me, and
I won't do it again.'*

*I said, 'It is too late now.' I was mad, and threw her back and struck
her, I believe, about the body. The last blow or two, I believe, was in
the neck with my knife. I made up my mind to do it dinner time, but
my brother was there. I put the razor and knife under the bed. I stayed
till daylight to write the letter before I tried to drown myself. I put
my coat and cap, with the letter and my watch, on a stone, and put
another stone on top of it, before I tried to drown myself.*

Frank Burden then raised his hands and showed them to
Captain Pretor, the chairman of the magistrates. On his
left hand were two cuts, both roughly an inch long, on the
palm of his left hand. There were also two cuts on his left

thumb. According to the accused man, these cuts had been done, 'through my wife drawing the razor out of my hand.' On his right fourth finger was another cut, 'done by my wife closing the knife across it.'

If this was a vague attempt to claim some sort of provocation or self-defence, it had little effect on the magistrates, who unanimously decided that Frank Burden would face trial at the Dorset Summer Assizes in June.

This would mean that the accused man was now required to spend more than three months on remand. However, the circumstances under which the crime was committed, together with Frank Burden's poor personal financial position, resulted in the Crown instructing Dr P W Macdonald, the Medical Superintendent of Dorset County Asylum, and Dr WE Good, the doctor at Dorchester jail, to examine and report on Frank Burden's mental state. The cost of these in-depth studies was to be financed by HM Treasury and would be declared at the accused man's trial.

Finally, the trial date arrived, Friday 6th June 1902. Coincidentally, on the same day, the newspapers were preoccupied with the recent discovery of the skeletons of five children, found at an address in Fishponds, Bristol. The cottage had previously been occupied by Mrs Amelia Dyer (mentioned in the chapter *The Angel Makers*). Amelia Dyer had been executed six years earlier for the murder of a child in her care.

Those in charge of law making in England, were perhaps distracted by this revelation, highlighting as it did, the failure of the authorities to act quickly enough against the horrors of baby farming. However, in the trial of Frank

Burden, there was to be no such sluggishness. Mr Justice
Bucknill had already stated his intention to complete the
proceedings as quickly as possible, allowing him a day's rest
before travelling to Wells. It was agreed between the judge
and both counsels that, due to the long period in which
Frank Burden had been under observation at Dorchester
Prison, the unusual step of firstly allowing full medical
reports to be entered in evidence would be permitted.

Dr Henley described the scene at No. 95 Reforne on 11th
February:

*I examined the body of the deceased in the bedroom shortly after six
o'clock. I found there the body of a well-nourished, well-developed
woman, about five feet eight in height, about twenty-five years old,
lying partly dressed on her back on the floor. The head was turned over
to the left, resting partly against the lower part of the back wall. The
hair was dressed and undisturbed. The back part of the hair, neck,
head, part of the shoulders, and back, were covered and lying in bright
red blood. The blood was fluid, and from it was issuing a vapour. The
eyelids were open and the eyeballs fixed. There was no life in the body.*

*The surface of the body was pale and blanched and quite warm, and
was covered on the front by a number of wounds. There were many
injuries to the body, to the navel, abdominal wall, bowels, breasts,
collarbone, neck, jaw, right internal jugular vein, right ear, armpit,
shoulder, elbow, hands and forearm. There were certain signs of
pregnancy.*

*The punctured wounds were such as might have been caused by a
pocket-knife, and the incised wounds could have been caused by a
razor. The incised wounds were probably caused in self-defence.
Probably the wounds in the neck were inflicted first, and after those, the
wounds in the abdomen.*

The first medical evidence regarding the condition of
Frank Burden came from Dr Peter Macdonald, the
Medical Superintendent at the Dorset County Asylum
in Charminster, known as Herrison Hospital. However,
because Burden had been classified as a 'Criminal Lunatic',
he was being kept at the more secure prison in Dorchester,
rather than at Herrison Hospital, requiring Dr Macdonald
to make a series of visits to Dorchester Prison.

The *Lunacy and County Asylum Act 1845* had been introduced
in an effort to treat mentally ill patients in well managed
and secure facilities. However, another major objective
of the *Act* had been to reclassify mentally ill workhouse
inmates as 'Pauper Lunatics', enabling them to be moved to
asylums. This had resulted in high levels of overcrowding
at Herrison Hospital, with patient numbers increasing
from 300 in 1860, to 472 in 1884, then 700 by 1902.
Although Dr Macdonald had many years' experience, due
to the resulting constraints on his time, he was only able
to observe Frank Burden on four occasions between 19th
February and his trial on 6th June. Whether this allowed him
to make an accurate diagnosis is debatable. Tasked with
accessing Burden's mental capacity during the actual act
of killing his wife, Dr Macdonald was not given access to
Burden until ten days after the tragedy. The evidence in the
letters written by Burden (mentioned previously) already
indicated that Frank Burden's mental state appeared to
have significantly changed between the rambling notes
written on the night of the murder, and the more coherent
letter to his parents two days later.

Before giving his testimony, Dr Macdonald, a proud
Scotsman, insisted on being sworn in using the Scottish

legal oath, rather than the traditional wording used in an English court of law. This caused much amusement in the public gallery, who were ordered to settle before the doctor could begin his statement:

I had been instructed by the Treasury to examine the prisoner and report on his mental state at the time of the commission of the crime. I saw him four times and had long examinations, extending from one-and-three-quarter hours to over two hours.

Physically, he is poorly or badly developed. His spine is not normal, nor were his thighs. Taken generally, he was stunted, and gave witness at the first examination, that his progenitors (ancestors) *must have had some disease which was likely to produce such results.*

When I first visited him in prison, I found that in the course of our conversation he would lose himself and become confused. His memory was defective. Burden told me that when he previously worked in glass-houses at Southampton, he had a sunstroke, and that ever since he had suffered from great pains in the head. He also added that the same pains were in his head on the day of the act.

He would only talk about his wife. I asked him about his condition prior to the commission of the crime. He then asked me, 'Did you know that I had killed my wife? But I did not know what I was doing: I felt so ill.'

I asked him if he still believed the statement he had made about his wife being unfaithful. He said, 'Oh yes; I am quite sure.' He repeated this many times. He also told me that he had seen the Devil enter the corner of his room on the previous night, and was so frightened he had jumped out of bed and paced about the room.

I found no evidence that his delusion regarding his wife was correct. It is a delusion which is well known amongst the class that, in my opinion, the prisoner belongs to, a class known as 'the mental and physical degenerates'.

I have also put together a family history of the prisoner and found very strong traces of insanity on both sides. His father's brother was insane, also his father's cousin. On his mother's side, I found his uncles and aunt had been insane. I have visited the prisoner twice during this present week, and I consider him to be still suffering the same symptoms, but in an aggravated form.

Therefore, from this information and from my own enquiry I have formed the opinion that, at the time of the act, he was suffering from a fixed delusion regarding his wife, and that he is of a weak mind, due to the long history of family insanity.

However, the next witness to be called, Dr William Good, the Medical Officer at Dorchester Prison, seemed to offer a very different opinion:

The prisoner was under my observation from February 19ᵗʰ. During the long period of his detention in Dorchester Gaol, he evinced no symptoms of insanity. I cannot speak to the prisoner's condition at the time of the murder. I have confined myself simply to his state since he had been under my observation.

The final expert witness, Dr Lionel Weatherley, a GP and attending doctor at Bailbrook Asylum, near Bath, stated that, 'The prisoner's delusion would be likely to induce a violent act – such as homicide or suicide, or both.' Although Dr Weatherley did think it likely that Burden's obsession with his wife's supposed infidelity might trigger a violent response, he appears to have stopped short of actually declaring Frank Burden insane.

Because the trial had begun unusually late on the Friday evening, and with the proceedings spilling over until early the following morning, Mr Justice Bucknill had clearly heard enough. He wasted no time in bringing the proceedings to a hasty conclusion. After thanking the witnesses, he addressed his final summation to the jury:

It would be a terrible thing, with the evidence before you, to send this prisoner to his doom. He is possessed with one of the most ordinary forms of insanity in that class of persons called degenerates – a class in whose family history there is a hereditary taint of insanity. Of course, the longer it went on, the more degenerate and weaker the family became. Then came some stress, then the awful deed. And there you are.

He waved his hand eloquently at the jury at this point, before continuing:

You will now return a verdict that the prisoner committed the deed, but that at the time of the offence he was suffering from insanity. Therefore, according to the law, he was not responsible for the act.

After just a few moments' deliberation the jury unanimously delivered the agreed verdict and Frank Burden was addressed by Mr Justice Bucknill:

Stand up. The verdict that is returned against you is that you are guilty of the act of murder, but that you were insane at the time. You will be kept in custody at Dorchester Prison, as a Criminal Lunatic, until the King's pleasure is known.

The trial finished at 10.30am, after having lasted a total of two-and-a-half-hours.

For the players in this tragic drama, there were to be no happy endings. Emily Burden was buried in the churchyard at St George's, just a short distance from the house in which she had been brutally murdered. Emily's mother Caroline Green, whose misguided but touching letter had attempted to reconcile the couple, continued to live with the knowledge that, had she persuaded Emily to leave her husband, her daughter's life may have been saved. Emily's mother carried that guilt for a further nineteen years before eventually passing away in 1921.

Frank Burden was finally released from the criminal lunatic wing of Dorchester Prison thirty-two years later, just before Christmas 1934, at the age of sixty-five. Unfortunately, he was unable to see his mother again. Fanny Burden had passed away just four years earlier at the age of eighty-eight, after hoping against hope that she might one day see her son released.

Frank Burden died five years later at his family home in Gutch Common, Semley, in Wiltshire, at the age of 70.

We are left with a burning question in this case, however. Did the bereaved family of Emily Burden receive justice for her death? Should Frank Burden have faced the hangman?

There are several inconsistences in both Frank Burden's behaviour and in his trial. Firstly, much of Frank Burden's conduct just prior to Emily's death suggests pre-planning and a cool calculating mind – locking the front door, hiding the knife and razor blade after the attack (after carefully closing the blades first), sliding the bolt on the back door, and then escaping. Did he really attempt to take his own life, or was it a carefully designed ruse? After all, he was rational enough to carefully place his handwritten notes, cap, and coat on a rock first. In addition, his lucid letter to his parents just two days later, seemed to indicate a much calmer and rational mind.

Burden's rather rushed trial seems rather at odds with his three months on remand when measured against his far lengthier magistrate's hearing in Weymouth, which had lasted almost eight hours and included many more witnesses.

The medical evidence was far from unanimous, with weight appearing to be given to the statements of Dr Macdonald, who met with Burden for a total of seven hours, rather than Dr Good, who had observed him daily for more than three months. The medical diagnosis also relied heavily on the hereditary possibility of the accused man having inherited his jealous delusions regarding his wife. In fact, the likelihood of genetically inheriting a condition from an uncle or aunt (as was supposed at this trial), is far less probable than one inherited from a parent, which does not seem to have been the case here.

It must also be remembered that Frank Burden showed no previous signs of mental illness, alcoholism, or erratic behaviour. His fixation on his wife's supposed infidelity came, not from within his own mind, but from remarks made to him by two independent sources.

Finally, at Burden's trial it was recorded in contemporary newspaper reports that even Burden's own defence barrister, Mr Charles Garland, was surprised that the prosecution counsel failed to press for a murder conviction; appearing to be satisfied with the direction of Mr Justice Bucknill.

Perhaps further scrutiny and a more in-depth trial may have led to a different verdict, one which would have greater satisfied Emily's grieving family. However, during the Edwardian era - as appears to be the case here - the justice system did not work to its full potential at the weekend.

LYME REGIS AND THE ONE-MAN CRIME WAVE

Do not do an immoral thing for moral reasons!

Thomas Hardy, *Jude the Obscure*, 1895

During the Great War, and directly following its conclusion, a baffling mystery perplexed the shopkeepers of Broad Steet, the hilly shopping thoroughfare in Lyme Regis.

Mr Leslie Haddon owned and managed two neighbouring shops in the town, at numbers 26 and 27 Broad Street. The premises, a gentlemen's outfitters and a draper's shop, were busy affairs, employing a total of twenty-five people. Opposite Haddon's was a long-established family greengrocer and wine merchants operated by Mr Frederick Burge. Beginning in 1915 and continuing until late 1920, all three shops were continually blighted by the unexplained disappearance of huge amounts of stock. Men's and ladies' clothing, umbrellas, hats, silks, and bales of cotton, from Haddon's. From Burge's grocery shop opposite, over 120 bottles of wine vanished. Along with cases of fruit, meat, fish, eggs, butter, sugar, candles and tobacco. In addition, other shops in Broad Street also reported missing and unaccounted for items seemingly vanishing from their premises – jewellery, china, glassware, silver, tools and provisions. Eventually, as the apparent thefts increased, a list was compiled at Lyme Regis police station. By 1920, the list had stretched to six pieces of foolscap paper, crammed on both sides with every available space filled, detailing the inordinate scale of the robberies. The total value of the goods amounted to more than £2,000 (today's equivalent of more than £135,000). In reality, the amount stolen was undoubtedly much higher, as not all the shops kept accurate and itemised stock records.

The two shopkeepers to have suffered the most, Leslie Haddon and Frederick Burge, were at a complete loss to explain the strange losses. Both men had fitted high-quality security locks to their shop's doors and windows, there had been no signs of forced entry, and Leslie Haddon even had an ex-policeman living as a tenant in the flat above 27 Broad Street.

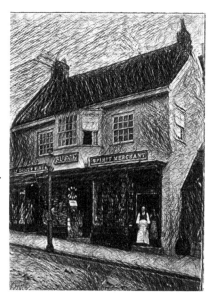

Both Mr Haddon and Mr Burge had for some time been unaware of the true scale of theft from their premises due to their involvement in the Great War. However, on returning to Lyme Regis after demobilisation, the sheer size of the losses became obvious. In January 1920, Mr Haddon decided to improve the shop's security and asked the ex-policeman living above his shop, Robert Ostler, to install new locks and strengthen the door and window frames in the shop and stockroom. Ostler, since retiring from the Railway Police, had earned a living as an odd job carpenter and decorator. His wife, Lizzie, had been bedridden for two years following an attack of paralysis. In fact, Ostler himself was not a physically fit man, who appeared to struggle to even carry his tools. Nevertheless, Leslie Haddon felt sorry for his tenant, knowing that he needed to care for his disabled wife.

With Robert Ostler now employed to enhance the security on the premises, Leslie Haddon felt a little safer.

One day, during January 1920, Mr Haddon closed both shops for the lunch hour, as was traditional. He locked the street facing doors to both shops and, as an added precaution, he also bolted the rear entrance. As usual, he closed the internal doors to the passageway that led to the two flats upstairs (although he did not lock these). However, on going upstairs to his flat, Mr Haddon realised he had left his newspaper in the shop; and went back downstairs to fetch it. On reaching the bottom of the stairs he noticed that both doors in the passageway were now open. He walked through into the drapery shop and found that the doors were unlocked. Yet, he distinctly remembered locking them. In fact, the key was still in the lock on the inside of the door, where he had left it minutes earlier. In the gentlemen's outfitting department, Mr Haddon's key was also still inside the lock on the inside of the door. He turned the handle and found to his astonishment that the door was unlocked. However, he was about to be greeted by an even bigger surprise. On the outside of the door, there was yet another key in the keyhole. As far as Leslie Haddon was aware, there were no other keys to the premises; he firmly believed he held the only set. Removing both sets of keys, he compared them. It appeared that the end of one key had been filed flat, reducing it in length and thus enabling it to be pushed into the keyhole and unlock the door, even if the key on the other side was already in the lock. Mr Haddon promptly removed the rogue key and hid it. He then turned and walked back through the shop.

As he passed the cellar entrance, he distinctly heard the unmistakable sound of someone moving about in the cellar below. He shouted down the cellar stairs, *Come up! I know who it is.*

Sure enough, Robert Ostler emerged sheepishly from the cellar. He was empty-handed, other than a small piece of wood in his right hand.

I knew it was you. Mr Haddon announced, *What are you doing down there?*

I came in for a piece of wood I needed. I knew it was down there, Robert Ostler answered.

You shouldn't be here.

Please overlook this, Mr Haddon. I need the work on account of my wife, Lizzie's, illness.

Leslie Haddon reluctantly agreed to overlook the matter but told Robert Ostler that as soon as his wife was better, he would need to give up the tenancy of the flat upstairs. Ostler agreed. Nonetheless, Mr Haddon took further steps and fitted extra sliding bolts to the inside of all the doors. Thinking that matters were now resolved, Mr Haddon continued as before, enforcing a new rule, that Ostler was no longer allowed to work in the shop, or even enter the premises. At least, the shopkeeper thought to himself, Ostler can longer steal goods from my shop.

However, despite the additional security measures, the puzzling thefts continued.

Unable to understand the reason behind the missing stock in his shops, Mr Haddon continued to ensure all the doors and windows were bolted and secured from the inside every night. Yet almost every morning, he would notice something else missing from the shops. Sometimes an umbrella or two, occasionally a hat, or even a piece of cloth cut from a roll of fabric. This continued on a regular basis for almost a year, until December 1920.

One evening during the Christmas holiday, two of Mr Haddon's shop assistants, Kathleen Hawker and Florence Searle, happened to be walking down Broad Street. As they passed the shop, a movement inside the premises caught their eye. Inside was the unmistakeable sight of Robert Ostler, helping himself to various items from the displays. Yet the doors to the shop were still locked and closed. They immediately knocked on the door of the adjacent flat and informed Leslie Haddon.

He angrily confronted Ostler and demanded to be given access to the ex-policeman's flat. Ostler reluctantly agreed and the party went inside. Sure enough, the rooms of Ostler's flat appeared like an Aladdin's Cave, awash with goods, boxes, and even money. Robert Ostler, of course, had little choice but to admit his landlord; perhaps he had hoped to persuade Haddon to be lenient once more. However, despite Lizzie Ostler's tears, this time Leslie

Haddon was in no mood to be forgiving. Instead, the police were called, and Robert Ostler was charged with theft.

There was intense local interest in the case. At Ostler's trial, at the historic Guildhall in Lyme Regis on Thursday 6th January 1921, crowds packed inside the hall and along Church Street and Bridge Street. The *Taunton Courier* set the scene perfectly:

The trial of Robert Ostler (64), charged with stealing goods valued at over £1,000, calculated to fill four large vans, took place at the Guildhall on Thursday. The case revealed some astounding discoveries made by the police and tradesmen, and has, as might be imagined, created much interest in the borough. The Guildhall was crowded to its utmost capacity. The accused man, who has been detained at Dorchester Jail since his arrest, was conveyed to the court in a motor van, accompanied by two warders. For eleven years past, Ostler has resided with his wife in rooms above the business premises of Mr Leslie Deacon Haddon, draper and outfitter, of Broad Street. By no means a robust man, it is marvellous that he was physically able to remove from shops in the town, the large quantity of articles, some of them of considerable weight, to his rooms. The charges are, without doubt, the most amazing that have been heard outside of London.

The importance of the case to the businesses of the town saw both the current and previous mayors sitting in judgement, Mr A Wiscombe and Mr A.J Woodroffe. Ostler was asked to sit near the packed press table. An upset and tearful Lizzie Ostler was also brought into court in a wheelchair to be at her husband's side. Since her husband's arrest, she had been moved to the home of a relative at Rocombe, near Uplyme.

The trial, which was to last more than four hours, began with Ostler being charged as follows:

Breaking and entering the premises of Leslie Deacon Haddon on December 26th and divers other dates, and stealing two large rolls of lino, several carpets, bundles of rugs and mats, numerous blankets, sheets, tablecloths, bales of shirts, umbrellas, rolls of silk, dresses, ready-made suits, overcoats, etc to the total value of £907 2s 7d.

He responded to the charge by announcing, *I have nothing to say.*

Mr Austen Whetham, who appeared for the prosecution, observed that the amount of goods recovered from Ostler's rooms:

Did not represent anything like the tally actually stolen, as Ostler had already disposed of a great deal of it. These robberies have been going on for a great many years, and with a great deal of cunning. About twelve months ago, when the accused man was found on Mr Haddon's premises in suspicious circumstances, he had bolts placed on the doors. The prisoner then cut a hole in the partition at the foot of the staircase leading to his rooms, through which he gained access to Mr Haddon's business premises.

After the two shop assistants employed by Mr Haddon saw the accused man at Christmastide, helping himself to various things in the shop, a subsequent search of his rooms found goods stored everywhere. One bedroom was, itself, like a drapery store. Goods were neatly packed away, wrapped in Mr Haddon's calico and labels. The searching of his rooms resulted in there being found a box containing £254 in notes (approximately £16,000 today). *There was also discovered two banking accounts, both with a credit of over £100. Another building society book showed a similar amount. All sorts of other things were uncovered – electric torches, a large number of files and keys, many of the latter having been filed to fit not just Mr Haddon's premises, but other locks in the town.*

Mr Haddon himself was called to give evidence. He described discovering another thirty men's shirts hidden in the coal cellar, and his confrontation with the accused man:

I pointed to the wooden partition and said, 'I feel convinced this is the way you got in.' On removing a picture, which hung on the partition wall, I found that two of the boards had been cunningly cut away, making enough room for a man to gain entry to my business premises on the other side. I also noticed that some of the goods taken from my shop dated as far back as 1915 or 1916.

Police Constable Cherrett was next to be interviewed. He confirmed that, on arresting Ostler, the accused man said to him, *It is quite right, I am very sorry. I have already admitted everything to Mr Haddon.*

Robert Ostler was then charged with breaking and entering the premises of Frederick Burge, Grocer and Wine Merchant. Mr Whetham continued for the Crown:

£165 worth of goods belonging to Mr Burge has been found at the accused's house. There is little doubt that the accused man has been practically living off goods that he stole from the shop. Although the accused man has never been employed at Mr Burge's shop, he was seen coming out of the door on the lower side of the shop. About twelve months ago, Mr Burge also fitted bolts to the door of his shop. However, when Mr Burge found that the woodwork had been cut away so that the bolt could be pushed back with a penknife, he had a padlock fitted instead. It then seems that the accused manufactured a key, which was found at his house, and used this to gain access to the shop.

When questioned, Robert Ostler denied taking any goods or money from Mr Burge's shop:

I have bought bottles of wine and whisky from Mr and Mrs Burge in the past, he testified, *I have never taken any cash from them. A good deal of the things claimed by Mr Burge were bought by my wife before the summer season opened, during when we had visitors. They were bought in London, though.*

Much to the amusement of the public gallery he then added, almost as an afterthought and obviously forgetting that he had previously denied stealing anything, *I should also like to say that I wish Mr Burge to have the goods back. I don't wish to see them again.*

Two further witnesses were then presented to the magistrates. Walter Wilson, a retired ironmonger, testified to seeing Ostler leaving Mr Burge's shop by the side door carrying a large basket. Samuel Glover, the Broad Street blacksmith, told the court that he had seen the accused man leaving the premises by a side door which he knew to be usually locked.

To heap more trouble on the accused man, Superintendent Beck of the Dorset Constabulary then confirmed that at least four further charges of theft would be applied for:

If the magistrates agree to send the accused to the Assizes, he stated, *these warrants will be brought to the notice of the prisoner on the 22nd inst. Many residents of the town have identified objects belonging to them, which were in the accused's possession. Mrs Escott, Mr W Wilson, Mr HE Foxwell, and Mr JF Hill are among those.*

Ostler again stated, *I have nothing to say.*

It appeared, according to evidence given by Superintendent Beck, that Robert Ostler had operated a staggering one-man crime wave in the town on an almost industrial scale. Over the previous decade he had stolen an estimated 'five or six hundredweight of goods', then sold them on to suppliers in London as legitimate merchandise. He had collected a significant amount of money from his efforts, yet it had taken many years before he had become a suspect. No doubt, his previous career as a policeman, his age, and his long-suffering wife's medical condition, made him immune from public suspicion. Ironically, despite committing hundreds, if not thousands, of robberies over almost ten years, he was never able to spend ostentatiously, for fear of becoming conspicuous. Nor could he move to a larger home and risk losing access to the Aladdin's Cave of treasures next door.

Ostler was convicted on all charges at the 1921 Dorset Winter Assizes in Dorchester and sentenced to four years' hard labour at Parkhurst Prison on the Isle of Wight. It was recommended that the Crown's costs be paid from Ostler's ill-gotten gains. The shopkeepers of Lyme Regis were far from happy, however, and did not feel that justice had been done in the case. Ostler's sentence was certainly remarkably light, especially considering the sheer scale of his criminal endeavours. Perhaps his age and his wife's paralysis played in his favour.

He served just over two years of his term, before being released early for good behaviour on 23rd April 1923. Tragically, he did not see his wife again, to whom he had been devoted. Lizzie had died just a few months after Ostler's imprisonment in 1921, at the age of just 51.

Robert Ostler lived a long life, however, and does not appear to have reoffended following his release. He eventually passed away in Rocombe, near Uplyme, on 29th March 1945 at the age of 88.

THE BODY UNDER THE BRIDGE
(PART ONE)

Friday 22nd April 1870 had been a lively day in the usually quiet Devon village of Colyford. The annual Steeple Chase meeting in nearby Colyton had drawn a large crowd to the area and the White Hart Inn was thronging with merry racegoers. It had been a busy day for the local police constable, Richard Walters, too. Just before 11pm he paid a visit to the White Hart Inn on Swan Hill Road. Although the inn was packed with noisy drinkers, a group of three particularly caught his attention. Two men and a woman were sat drinking on the settle in the kitchen. The constable recognised the two men. One was James Pepperell, a thirty-six-year-old farm labourer from the village of Membury. The other was James Harris, a labourer from Lyme Regis. PC Walters did not recognise the woman. Both men seemed merry, but not drunk, although the woman appeared to be heavily intoxicated. As the hour for closing had now passed, the landlord requested the constable's help in escorting the trio from the Inn.

The policeman politely asked the three to leave, telling them it was now closing time. James Pepperell stood up and paid for the drinks with a half-sovereign coin, putting the change in his money purse afterwards. He appeared, on doing this, to be rather the worse for drink than the constable's first impression had been. The other man, James Harris, got up, without speaking and left the inn immediately. Several of the customers inside the inn noticed that he was carrying a heavy walking stick as he did so. Harris turned right and headed east out of the village towards Lyme Regis.

After five minutes or so PC Walters, Pepperell, and the woman all left the White Hart Inn. Outside the door, they said goodbye. Walters and the woman turned left into the village and Pepperell took the same route as Harris had done five minutes earlier, heading east towards the Axe River on the road to Lyme Regis. The policeman watched him walk off into the darkness, past the railway station, around the curve in the road, and out of sight. It would be the last time anyone saw James Pepperell alive.

Pepperell was not reported missing immediately. He lived alone and frequently did not return to his lodgings for days at a time.

Eleven days later, on Tuesday 3rd May 1870, PC Walters was asked to investigate a possible sighting of a body in the River Axe, underneath the Axe Bridge, just outside Colyford. Collecting a rope and iron crook from the village on the way, he walked the half-mile east from Colyford until he reached the narrow bridge over the river. A small crowd had already gathered there. Scrambling down under the bridge and using the iron crook, he was able to drag the object to the bank. It was, indeed, a body.

Although decomposition had begun, the corpse was still intact. It was assumed that the victim had sunk and then re-floated after the gases in the chest had caused the body to swell. This may account for the fact that no one had noticed it before. PC Walters did not initially recognise the body as that of James Pepperell, although this was later remedied. At this stage Pepperell had still to be reported missing, so the constable had no immediate link between the identity of the body and a suspected missing person.

As was the usual practice in these circumstances, a coroner's inquest was called to determine the cause of death, and a jury and witnesses were summoned. Mr SM Cox, the Devon Deputy Coroner, appointed Captain Dick as foreman of the jury and the inquest opened on Thursday 5th May at the White Hart Inn, a matter of half-a-mile from the crime scene. The inquest took place in a small room at the front of the inn. It was overcrowded, hot, and stuffy. Interest in the case had been acute in Colyford and every available space in the room was occupied. Those who could not gain access to the room crowded in the passageway outside or peered through the window.

As the last person known to have seen James Pepperell alive, James Harris was arrested in Lyme Regis and placed in the cells overnight, before being escorted to the inquest by two police constables. The inquest was not a criminal court of law. Although a cause of death and verdict could be determined, a trial would still be required to secure a conviction. No lawyers were present and James Harris, unlike in a High Court trial, would be invited to cross-examine any of the witnesses, if he chose to do so.

Firstly, and most importantly, to open the proceedings a cause of death needed to be established. Had James

Pepperell been murdered, or was his demise merely an unfortunate accident? Dr John Snook, the surgeon from Colyton, was asked to give the results of his post-mortem:

On Tuesday evening I was called in to see the body of the deceased. He had evidently sustained serious injuries, and had received contusions about the face, forehead and neck. The body had apparently been a long time in the water, I should say ten days.

In the left trouser pocket, I found a sixpence, one halfpenny, a pocketbook, a small black purse, which was empty, and a few matches. In his coat pocket were two pipes and some tobacco. I found the body to be that of a fine muscular man, with no obvious illnesses, apparently about thirty years of age. There were no injuries on any parts of the body, other than the forehead, face, eyes, and each side of the neck. The left eyelid was cut through, as was a portion of one ear. The injuries had undoubtedly been caused by repeated blows from a heavy object. There was no congestion at all in his lungs, so that death could not have been caused by accidental drowning. A blow such as the deceased must have received under the left ear was sufficient in itself to cause death. I am satisfied that he was killed before he was thrown into the water.

At this point in the inquest a large and heavy stick, which had been found lying in a nearby field, was produced by the coroner:

Doctor, could the injuries sustained by the victim have been caused by such a stick?

Yes, such a stick would have likely caused the injuries.

James Pepperell's movements on the day of his disappearance were then investigated.

His landlady, Mrs Elzabeth Boyling, confirmed that Pepperell had rented a room at her cottage in Membury (a village ten miles to the north of Colyford) for the past ten years:

He left his lodgings with me at around seven o'clock on the morning of Colyton Steeplechases. He told me that he intended to spend the day at the races. I was not especially concerned when he did not return, as he regularly went away for ten or more days at a time and on occasion would come back tipsy; and I never knew him travel anywhere without money. He sometimes went out with a pocket-watch too, but I don't know if he wore it to the races that day. I have also never seen him in the company of James Harris before.

Pepperell was subsequently witnessed at the racecourse by a sailor named Alfred Stone, from Uplyme, who testified that Pepperell:

was full of life and vigour. He appeared to have some money about him, for I saw at least two half-sovereigns (approximately £160 today). *He had a black money-purse with a piece of elastic round it, which he took out to pay for some beer. I left him about six o'clock, and up to that time he did not seem the worse for liquor, and he had not picked up with any other acquaintances.*

Mr Pepperell wanted me to stay with him. He told me he had plenty of money, and that he would treat me to what I liked, if I would keep him company.

Mr Stone, did Mr Pepperell say where he was going that night, after the public house closed?

No, sir. He did not say where he was going. If he had, I could have taken him in my trap as far as Uplyme.

And you were previously acquainted with the deceased man, Mr Stone?

Yes, I worked with Pepperell at Wear Farm about two years ago. He then earned nine shillings a week as a carter.

At this point in the inquest, James Harris was asked if he wished to put any questions to the witness. Although the accused man was a powerfully built man of thirty, he appeared quiet and mild-mannered during the inquest. He shook his head initially, then changed his mind and said, *How was he about drinking? Did he go about drinking in excess?*

Alfred Stone was unable to confirm that the deceased man was a habitual drinker, and James Harris returned to his seat.

The next testimony came from the landlord of the White Hart Inn, John Quick, who confirmed that he had seen the deceased man enter his inn shortly after 9pm:

Soon after that, a woman named Sutton and a man named Harris also came in. The three sat drinking together, until eleven clock, the time for closing. Pepperell paid for the drink as Harris didn't appear to have any money. Pepperell was rather the worse for liquor, but not by any means incapably drunk. I noticed that Harris had a large stick with him in the public house, but I cannot swear what kind of one it was. At eleven o'clock, with the help of Constable Walters, I told the parties to leave the house.

Constable Walters was then asked to describe in detail the location at which the body was discovered:

The body was discovered in the River Axe, under Axe Bridge. The bridge is almost within sight of the White Hart Inn and the railway station. And Mr Fowler's farmhouse, and the tollgate are each within a few hundred yards of it. It is an ordinary country bridge, with only low side walls, so that a heavy weight might be easily pitched over by a moderately powerful man. The river is tidal, and at this point is twenty feet deep.

Constable, did you witness the deceased man arguing with anyone during your time in the White Hart Inn? enquired Mr Cox, the Deputy Coroner.

No, sir. I heard no quarrelling among his party. I did see a large stick in Harris's hand while he was drinking though. It was about the size of a hurdle stick.

Joshua Richards had been stood outside the White Hart Inn on the night in question, and he too witnessed James Harris leave, with James Pepperell following a few minutes later:

I saw the direction the parties went, he told the inquest, *when Harris came out of the inn, he went towards Axe Bridge. I heard his footsteps as far as the railway station, but I then lost the sound rather suddenly. James Pepperell came out a few minutes later with a woman, he also went towards Axe Bridge. The woman went the other way towards Colyton. I last saw her about ten minutes later, at Hilly Close Gate, about a quarter of a mile from the White Hart.*

Unlike a Victorian court trial, an inquest jury (as well as
being expected to view the body of the deceased), were
allowed to take an active part in the proceedings. Captain
Dick, the foreman of the jury, interrupted Joshua Richards
at this point in his testimony:

*Mr Richards, do you think you would usually be able to hear footsteps
from further away than the railway?*

Yes, sir, I thought I could hear footsteps further.

However, several of the jury members, all local men,
disagreed, remarking that a person would not hear the
sound of someone any further away than the railway gate.
Captain Dick thought the point an important one and
pressed the witness Joshua Richards again:

*Mr Richards, do you think, then, that you could not hear any more
footsteps because James Harris stopped at that point, or walked on?*

I could not say, sir.

Mr Cox, the coroner, interrupted and reminded the jury
that they should not ask the witness to guess, but make
their own judgement, based only on the evidence. He asked
Joshua Richards to continue his statement:

*Then, sir, the next morning, about six, I passed the bridge and saw
marks as if a scuffle had taken place in the road. There were no traces
of blood, but the gravel had been kicked about. It drew my attention,
but I did not think more about it until the body was found.*

Mr Simon Fowler, of Boswell Farm, was next to be
questioned. His evidence seemed important and appeared
to point strongly at Harris as the man guilty of Pepperell's
death:

Boswell Farm occupies the high ground within sight of the bridge. At quarter to six on the morning of the 23rd April (the morning after the last known sighting of James Pepperell), *I saw James Harris in my cowhouse; he got up from a crib in which he had apparently been sleeping. There was a bag at the other end, which he took with him. Harris said he had overslept, he had been to the races, and had come in to sleep. I told him to leave. When he got outside, he paused a little, looked about, and appeared rather uncertain which way to go. He had no stick with him at that time.*

PC Chapple, from Lyme Regis, stated that:

On Thursday, the 5th May, I went to Harris's house. When he saw me at the door, Harris said, 'I know what you want to find out, about the man that's drowned.' I had not then told him about the body in the river. He admitted to me that he had been to the races, and that he then came through Colyford, and that he drank there with a man he used to know in Membury called Pepperell. He added that he had been told that Pepperell was the man that had been drowned in Colyford.

I then charged him with the wilful murder of James Pepperell and gave him the usual caution as to his making any statement, and Harris then said to me:

'It isn't me that done it, sir. On the night of the races, I came home to Lyme Regis, where I arrived at about two or three o'clock in the morning, just as it was daylight.'

He also further said to me, 'This is a bad job, I wish I had stayed home from the races altogether, I don't like being in these messes'.

Next to be investigated was the perplexing question of the mysterious woman seen in the White Hart with James Harris and James Pepperell. Constable Walters confirmed that he had walked with her from the White Hart Inn, *as far as Coles' Mills. I left her walking towards Colyton. I then came back to Colyton Cross and went up Colyford Street. She was out of my sight.*

It emerged that the mysterious woman had told Harris and Pepperell that her name was Sutton. However, no one recognised the name and she seemed to have disappeared since the night of the murder. It was decided to adjourn the inquest, as she may hold vital information in the case.

A notice was placed in several newspapers in an effort to trace her whereabouts:

THE MURDER NEAR SEATON

A woman who goes by the name of Sutton, who was in the company of the now deceased James Pepperell and the prisoner James Harris at the White Hart Inn, Colyford, on the night of 22nd of April, is required at the Coroner's Inquest into the death of the above, at the White Hart Inn, by JL Scarborough, Esq, and Mr SM Cox (Deputy Coroner, Devon)

The woman in question was eventually located in Barnstaple. She had used the alias Sutton, although her married name was Lizzie Gunn. After sleeping off the excesses of the Colyton Steeple Chase, somewhere in Colyford, she had returned to Barnstaple the following day, probably assuming her husband would have been less than pleased to discover she had spent the evening at the White Hart with two other men! She was immediately conveyed to Colyford and the inquest recommenced. She was, however, unable to add much to the proceedings, stating only that:

Pepperell paid for the whole of the liquor we drank. Harris said that he had no money. After that I went straight to Colyton, but I cannot remember where I slept. Then I went home to Barnstaple.

The forced delay to the inquest did allow Mr Simon Fowler (the farmer who had discovered Harris sleeping in his barn on the morning after Pepperell disappeared) to recall a crucial detail:

Since my first appearance here, I have had time to think again about the night when the parties left the White Hart. My farmhouse faces Axe Bridge, and is perhaps less than a quarter of a mile from it. On the night of the Colyton Races, I went to bed rather late. About twenty minutes before twelve I heard cries coming from the direction of Axe Bridge.

Although I thought little of it at the time, on reflection I consider they were like the cries of a man in distress. At first, they were very loud. I said to my wife, 'There's someone hollering pretty well on Axe Bridge tonight!' After hearing the cries three times she replied, 'It's the people returning from the races.' We heard the sound three or four more times, but in a lower tone. If it had been any other night than that of the races, I should have taken more notice. But considering that there would be then a great many drunken people about, I did not consider it worthwhile to go down. I regret now that I did not. I thought, perhaps, it might have been a drunken brawl, and that one of the party was getting the worst of it and was calling for help. The sound was exceedingly loud for the first three or four cries; then lower after that. The wind was blowing strongly from the west towards my house that night, perhaps that is why I could hear it so clearly.

Captain Dick thought Mr Fowler's remark about the direction of the wind an important one, and directed a comment of his own towards the coroner:

The direction of the wind would prevent anybody in the village hearing the cries. I keep a dog loose on my property and I do not recollect noticing the animal being disturbed by any unusual noise.

Another witness, Samuel Larcombe, the tollkeeper at the Axmouth Gate, also came forward to state that he did not hear any unusual noise on the night in question:

I live at the Tollhouse, which is about a couple of hundred yards from Axe bridge. I went to bed about twelve o'clock, but I did not recollect anybody in particular passing along the road. I did hear footsteps at different times; but I did not hear any noise or cry. If there had been loud cries on the bridge, I think I should have heard them. My house is between the bridge and Mr Fowler's farmhouse. It lays in a hollow, and Boswell Farmhouse lies on the hill.

Captain Dick asked: *Mr Larcombe, do you think it possible for sounds to be heard at Boswell Farm, and not at your house?*

Larcombe replied: *It is possible, yes, for the sound would go quite over my house.*

Mr Cox thanked him and asked James Harris if he wished to cross-examine Mr Fowler or Mr Larcombe. Harris nodded and mumbled to Mr Fowler:

I had a drop to drink that night, and being tired, I went in the shed to lie down. I heard no cries.

That is a statement, Mr Harris, not a question. Do you have one that you wish to ask this witness?

No, sir.

The next part of the inquest would see an emotional appearance from the victim's father, a move hardly likely to help James Harris's case…

THE BODY UNDER THE BRIDGE
(PART TWO)

John Pepperell, the father of the deceased man, appeared tired and emotional as he answered the coroner's questions. He informed the inquest that he had been staying at his son's lodgings in Membury to assist with the enquiry:

Since the news was given to me, I have been going through my son's things. His working clothes were there, but no money. I do not know what he earned, but he always had plenty of money to carry him backwards and forwards. When he came to see me last, he had a sovereign, a half-sovereign, and silver in his possession.

George Hore, a miller from Lexhayne Mills near Axminster, told the inquest that:

On the morning after the races I saw a man, whom I believe to be James Harris. He also told me that his name was Harris. He was lying on the bank of a field on Crabhayne Farm, about eleven o'clock in the morning.

I said to him, 'Well, my friend, you've had bit of a nap, then?'

Harris replied, 'Yes, I have, but I'm very cold.'

He then stood up. I said to him, 'You've been to the races, I suppose?'

Harris replied that he had, and, said that he 'had taken a little drop too much last night, and was very dry.'

I asked him how he came to be lying there, and he replied, 'I don't know, nor do I know where I am now. I'm supposed to be looking for work.'

Harris kept complaining that he was thirsty, and I said that if he would come with me to the White Hart, which was about half a mile away, I would buy him a pint of beer. He replied, 'I don't know about going with you. I'll take off this here' he said, touching his slop (rough outdoor working clothing), *'or they'll say I'm a rough looking fellow.'*

Harris then followed me along the road and, when we came to Axe Bridge, Harris looked over the side of the bridge on the south side as we passed across it. When we came to the White Hart, I gave Harris a pint of beer, then I left him there.

At this point the coroner interrupted the witness to clarify two points:

Mr Hore, did you not notice anything particular about his slop? Did you also observe if he had a bag.

No sir.

And you did see a stick lying in the field?

Yes, sir. It was similar to a kidney-bean stick. (a cane with a heavy, curved handle)

And you have no doubt the prisoner stood here today was the man you met that morning?

No doubt, sir.

James Harris interjected loudly at this juncture, much to the chagrin of the coroner. His point, however, was a legally important one:

He never saw the stick in my hand though. The one he saw was lying on the ground. It could have been anyone's.

Mrs Emma Quick, the landlady of the White Hart, was called to testify next. She was able to confirm much of the evidence given by her husband and other witnesses, having seen James Harris on both the night before and the morning after James Pepperell's demise:

The three of them were drinking together. I could not swear that Harris had a stick, but I believe I saw him resting on one. Pepperell paid for all the drink and I heard no quarrelling between them.

At this juncture, the money-purse found by Constable Walters on the body of James Pepperell was shown to Mrs Quick:

Mrs Quick, is this the purse you saw the deceased man use in your public house on the night of his death?

I could not positively swear to it, sir. I thought the one I saw had elastic around it and a steel clasp. But it is a common enough one, that it could be. Perhaps the elastic got lost in the water?

Perhaps, Mrs Quick. This is certainly a common type of purse and, as you may see, it has a steel clasp. Please continue your statement.

Yes, sir. The woman named Sutton in their company was very drunk. Walters, the policeman, came in about five minutes to eleven, and we asked him to stop until the house was clear. Two other customers, George Hooper and William Hazell were also in the room. Constable Walters told the others it was time to drink up and leave, and Harris got up and went out instantly. That was, I should say, about ten minutes after eleven. He went towards Axe Bridge. All the rest went out together, between five and ten minutes afterwards. The woman and the policeman went towards Colyford village, and Mr Pepperell went towards Axe Bridge.

The next morning about eleven o'clock, Harris came to the house again, with Mr George Hore, the latter treated him to a pint of ale. I should think he stayed there for two hours or so. I asked him if he was the man who was there the previous night, and he said he was. I remember that the man had on a dirty slop, and he took it off and put it on the back windowsill. He said to me,

'I haven't been home last night. I've laid down over there.' He pointed through the window to the fields down the road.

'You've had a rough bed, then?', I said to him.

'I have', he answered. He then laid his head upon the table and appeared to go to sleep.

The slop and heavy walking-stick were then produced in court and shown to the next witness, William Hazell, a platelayer for the London and South-Western Railway, who had been in the public house the previous evening and was also acquainted with James Harris:

Do you recognise these items, Mr Hazell?

I could not swear to it that they are the same ones, sir. Although, when I saw him at the White Hart, he did have a stick in his hand. He spoke to me, saying that he knew me. He said that he had to go to Lyme Regis that night.

And do you recognise this stick, Mr Hazell?

I could not swear to it, sir. I fancy that the stick Harris had with him had a little knob on the top of it and was smaller the bottom.

Considering the short length of time between the
discovery of James Pepperell's body in the river and the
commencement of the inquest, the efficiency in gathering
witnesses is remarkable, especially as communication was
only possible by post, word of mouth, or the recently
introduced telegraph network. Next to speak was Miss
Fowler, daughter of the farmer Simon Fowler, who also
resided close to the Axe Bridge at Boswell Farm. She
recollected the events on the night of the Colyton Races:

*I went to bed about half-past eleven, and about ten minutes after I
heard loud cries coming from the direction of Axe Bridge. The noise
lasted altogether about a minute. Miss Grattan, a friend who was
staying with me, also heard the sounds, and asked what it was. I
replied that it was people returning from Colyton Races. The noise did
not frighten me, but had it been another occasion, it would have.*

Perhaps the most compelling piece of medical evidence
produced at the inquest was saved for last. The slop, which
James Harris had left on the windowsill of the White Hart
Inn on the following day, had been examined by Dr Snook,
at the request of Superintendent Dore of the Devon police.
In addition, a shirt also worn by the accused man was
produced. Superintendent Dore had noticed some dark
spots and some other marks on the clothing.

James Harris, when asked to account for the dark spots,
explained, *that is rabbit's blood. I caught a young rabbit the other
day. It's rabbit.*

The doctor was then asked for his opinion on the other
marks, *Dr Snook, have you examined the marks upon the clothing?*

*Yes. There were spots on the left sleeve of the shirt, but I could not say
what they were.*

James Harris was then given the chance to explain what might have caused the marks. He answered confidently, *Anybody could easily see what they are. They were caused when grafting trees.*

And the marks on your slop?

Like I said, that was a rabbit I caught. I never hurted the poor man. I am innocent.

Thank you, Mr Harris. Now, Dr Snook, will you give us your expert opinion on these marks?

Yes. The marks were dry and did not appear recent. With reference to the spots of blood, there is very considerable difficulty with it. The prisoner has admitted that it was blood, saying that it was from a rabbit. Sometimes by analysis and investigation, the medical profession are able to throw considerable light upon such matters, but I am afraid such light will not be forthcoming in this instance.

Dr Snook then produced a copy of *Taylor's Medical Jurisprudence*. This extensive journal, which often formed the basis of medical evidence in Victorian trials, was written by Alfred Swaine Taylor, a leading toxicologist and medical writer, who has often been dubbed the 'father of British forensic medicine'. In the introduction to his own book, Taylor describes the volume as being:

Firmly established as the work of ultimate reference in Courts of Law, designed to assist legal officers and medicolegal officials in the pursuit of their duties, with special reference to English customs, practice, regulations, and laws.

Dr Snook then quoted from his copy of the tome:

It is very easy to distinguish the difference between the blood of fishes and birds, and that of man, but it is not easy to tell the blood of man from that of quadrupeds. The only difference was in the size of the corpuscles of the blood, and unfortunately, the dog, the rabbit and the hare, were those which most nearly resembled that of man.
Dr Taylor also states: *that when blood is dried on clothing it cannot be distinguished between that of ordinary animals, and that of a human being.*

In fact, a test to accurately distinguish human blood from animal blood would not be developed until 1901. This procedure, known as the Specis Precipitin Test, was developed by a German scientist named Paul Uhlenhuth. A brilliant microbiologist, he would go on to be nominated for the Nobel Prize for Medicine on no less than forty occasions, until his career later became mired by his involvement in the experiments of the Nazi regime. As a young man, however, by reading about cases such as the death of James Pepperell, his discovery changed the face of criminal trials in the twentieth century and prevented many miscarriages of justice.

Meanwhile, returning to 1870, there was to be no such degree of certainty afforded to the mystery surrounding the death of James Pepperell.

Mr Cox, the Coroner, then thanked everyone for their evidence and expressed his opinion on the case to the jury:

It is quite clear that the prisoner had a stick, and to that extent he has been lying during these proceedings. It does not seem that there was any spite or quarrelling between the two parties, but on the contrary,

*it seems there was good feeling. It might at first have been thought that
they quarrelled over the woman, but that hypothesis was knocked over
as she was seen going in a different direction by Constable Walters.*

*If the accused has committed this murder, then it must have been for
money. The theory must be that he laid in wait for the deceased, but
it must be borne in mind that he left the public house first and did not
definitely know whether the deceased intended to travel that way or not.
Witnesses have come forward to show that Pepperell had money that
night, but not to show that Harris knew that he had any; although he
may have seen Pepperell's money-purse.*

*Mr Fowler's evidence, corroborated as it was with that of his
daughter, is most important, and shows that there was something
wrong going on that night on Axe Bridge. Coupling the cries heard
with the time the deceased left the public house, there can be very little
doubt that those cries came from the man being murdered. That the
man was foully dealt with there could be no doubt, but the question
was, by whom?*

*The prisoner told another lie about having gone home to Lyme Regis
on the night of the races. He had told two lies, that he had not a stick,
and that he had gone to Lyme. That is suspicious, but of course not
conclusive. Yet, it does seem singular that the man should stay about
the place of a murder instead of removing himself from it.*

*I do not think anything can be made out of the blood on his clothing.
It does seem extraordinary that there was so little blood to be seen. Yet,
Dr Snook said the deceased had no wound about him which would
give off a large amount of blood.*

*James Harris, do you wish to say anything before I ask the jury to
reach a verdict?'*

The prisoner replied, *I have nothing to say, sir, because I don't know anything about it. I am a married man with four children. I never hurted the man.*

The coroner then instructed the all-male jury:

Members of the jury, the question for you to decide here, is whether there is a sufficient prima facie case to send this man for trial to the next Assizes. Please retire and consider your verdict.

The room was duly cleared, and after twenty minutes' deliberation, the jury returned a verdict of 'Wilful Murder against James Harris'. and he was then committed to take his trial at the next Assizes.

The trial of James Harris was scheduled for Thursday 28th July 1870, at the Devon Lammas Assizes in Exeter. A large crowd gathered in anticipation of the pageantry surrounding the opening of the Assizes and the prospect of a murder trial. However, there was to be a remarkable twist in the tale.

James Harris pleaded 'Not guilty', to murder. However, at that precise moment, the prosecution barrister handed a piece of paper to the presiding judge, Mr Justice Willes:

It has been intimated to me by the Crown, that the evidence against the prisoner Harris is not sufficient to warrant any further proceedings and that the Grand Jury would come to the same conclusion. The bill is thrown out. Prisoner at the bar, you are free to go.

This extraordinary timing of this development came as a complete surprise to James Harris. It can only be concluded that the Crown had assumed that Harris, terrified by the prospect of the impending death penalty, might enter a last-minute plea of guilty. Without that, they clearly believed, a conviction could not be obtained.

Nevertheless, short of extracting a cast-iron confession from the accused person, or obtaining a string of reliable eyewitness accounts detailing the actual killing, almost all Victorian murder convictions were gained using what today might be termed 'circumstantial evidence'. In the case of James Pepperell, the evidence (using the Victorian standard) seems to be strong indeed. Without the benefit of DNA, CCTV, fingerprints, or forensic science, the burden of proof required by the prosecution at trial usually relied on the cumulative effect of many layers of 'circumstantial evidence', rather than the absolute knowledge of, for example, a DNA match.

James Harris was the last known person seen with the murdered man. He hurriedly left the inn before the victim, yet his footsteps were heard stopping by the bridge. Did he lie in wait for Pepperell at a quiet spot near the bridge, knowing that the deceased man was carrying a money purse and was probably intoxicated? The coroner implied that Harris could not have known in which direction Pepperell would be walking when he left the inn, but it was highly probable that the two men had discussed their plans during their time in the public house. That is a far more likely contingency than a random stranger attacking Pepperell. After all, a stranger would not have known that Pepperell had a money purse, and could just as easily have robbed Harris instead.

James Harris also misled the police on at least two occasions. Firstly, claiming that he had returned to Lyme

Regis on the night of the attack and, secondly, denying that he had a large stick in his possession. The evidence of the stick is most important, since it appears to match the weapon used to attack James Pepperell. Several witnesses confirmed seeing Harris with a stick. One was also found the following morning, close to where he had slept. In addition, the multiple witnesses who overheard cries coming from the direction of Axe Bridge on the night of James Pepperell's disappearance, make it almost certain he was killed at that time. No one, other than James Harris, was seen near the bridge, either on the night of the murder, or the following morning.

The excuses given by Harris to explain the presence of blood on his clothing also seem a little too convenient. Had the trial taken place just three decades later, in the era of more sophisticated testing, a very different outcome might have been achieved.

So, there was to be no justice for the family of James Pepperell. James Harris walked free from Exeter Crown Court, and a short time afterwards he disappeared from Lyme Regis. He later resurfaced in London where he obtained employment as a painter and decorator.

An editorial in the *Exeter and Plymouth Gazette* lamented the failure of the authorities to convict Harris and also commented on their inability to solve three other murders which had recently occurred in the county.

Had the police delved a little deeper, they might also have discovered that James Harris had at least three previous convictions. He had been found guilty of poaching in Stalbridge in 1867, the robbery of a public house in

Southampton in 1868, and, most interestingly of all, robbery with violence in Weymouth in 1866. An assault in which the victim was attacked with a large walking-stick.

Several years later, in 1882, Harris was also convicted of robbery in Wandsworth. His apparent escape from justice in Devon does not appear to have prompted a change in his behaviour.

WITH THE SHORE SO NEAR
(THE BEGINNING)

In a solitude of the sea,
Deep from human vanity,
And the Pride of Life that planned her, stilly couches she.

Thomas Hardy, *The Convergence of the Twain*
(Lines on the Loss of the Titanic), 1912

As 1914 drew to a bitterly cold close, the real horrors of the Great War had yet to truly impact the town of Lyme Regis, nestled in Lyme Bay on the Jurassic Coast, sandwiched beneath the Dorset hills and the waters of the English Channel.

Optimistic hopes that the fighting would be 'over by Christmas' had not materialised and the townsfolk of Lyme Regis began to console themselves with the thought that the conflict was at least being fought on a distant shore, or in the far-off shipping lanes of South America and the North Sea. Rationing and conscription were not yet in force and, despite the wartime blackout regulations and regular clusters of battleships patrolling menacingly in the bay, day-to-day life continued in Lyme Regis for those not directly involved in the struggle.

Since the declaration of war on 4th August, British losses had been heavy. 1,600 men at Mons in the early days of the conflict. 1,400 lost on 22nd September when German U-boat U-9 had attacked three British ships in the waters off Ostend, and the loss of the entire crew of 900 when the Imperial German Navy sank *HMS Good Hope* in November off the coast of Chile, during the Battle of Coronel.

However, as dawn broke on Friday 1st January 1915, the cruel realities of the conflict finally reached even this sheltered corner of Dorset.

It was a tempestuous and bitterly cold New Year's Day, one which would live long in the memory of the townsfolk of Lyme Regis. Along with the courageous fishermen of the Devon coast, it would also be a day on which they would respond magnificently to the unexpected challenge that faced them.

HMS Formidable, a lead ship in her class of pre-Dreadnought battleships, had already become accustomed to danger during the early weeks of the war. The 14,500-ton vessel, equipped with midship armour plating, two triple-expansion steam engines, thirty-two guns, and four torpedo tubes, had helped protect the crossing of the British Expeditionary Force in August 1914, as part of the 5th battalion, and then guarded against the possibility of German invasion from her base at Sheerness in Kent. Yet there was to be no Christmas break for the crew of around 750 men, as the 5th battalion were ordered to take part in gunnery exercises off the Isle of Portland.

Under the command of Vice-Admiral Sir Lewis Bayly (Commander of the Channel Fleet), the *Formidable* spent

New Year's Eve engaged in exercises in the channel
off Portland, alongside *HMS London, Prince of Wales,*
Implacable, Queen, Agamemnon and *Lord Nelson.* The fleet was
accompanied by two light cruisers, *Topaze* and *Diamond.*
With winds freshening and storms forecast, the vessels
remained on patrol at the westernmost end of Lyme Bay,
approximately twenty miles from Start Point. Although
German submarine activity was suspected in the area,
Vice-Admiral Bayly expected no imminent threat due to
the anticipated stormy weather conditions and he decided
that no antisubmarine destroyer escort would be needed,
for what was merely a training exercise. In any case, surface
detection of U-boats was severely hampered by the rough
seas.

Rather than opting for a 'battle-ready' formation, Bayly
instead ordered the seven battleships to continue westward
in a 'line ahead' configuration (end-to-end, 400 metres
apart), proceeding at a light cruising speed of just ten knots.
HMS Formidable took up the final position in the line of

seven battleships, with just the two lightly armed cruisers astern. Known as the 'coffin position' by superstitious sailors, the ship would be the least protected of the seven larger vessels. Little did the crew of the *Formidable* know, the German submarine U-24 had been silently stalking the vulnerable fleet for several hours, patiently waiting for the optimum time and position to launch its deadly torpedo attack.

At midnight the Royal Navy's traditional sixteen-bell salute was rung onboard the *Formidable*. It was a brilliant full moon as the crew celebrated the new year. However, even as the crew retired to their bunks, the wind was strengthening. The swells grew in ferocity and rain began to lash the decks of the battleship as the moon disappeared behind thick cloud cover. Perfect conditions in which a submarine might go undetected.

Meanwhile, approximately 1,200 feet off the ship's starboard bow in the icy cold waters of Lyme Bay, U-24 carefully manoeuvred into a firing position. The U-Boat's commander, Kapitänleutnant Rudolf Schneider, was fortunate that Vice-Admiral Bayly's decision to order the British vessels to steam at only ten knots had enabled the slower submarine to match the *Formidable*'s speed and turns, until the battleship finally fell into U-24's torpedo range.

It is hard for anyone on land to imagine the utter and complete darkness of that stormy night. No moon or starlight could penetrate the swirling thick cloud that lashed down torrential rain and freezing hail, driven by the storm force winds, onto the rough and shifting seas. The normally welcoming and twinkling lights from the settlements around

Lyme Bay had been extinguished since October, as part of the wartime home defence regulations. Even the guiding arc of light from the Start Point lighthouse was now under Admiralty control. No coastal light that might aid enemy shipping was permitted. Although in the howling storm the horizon lookout on the *Formidable* would have struggled to make out anything other than the faint impression of the other ships as they steamed in convoy, rolling and pitching with each huge wave.

At a distance of 1,200 feet and closing, Kapitänleutnant Rudolf Schneider ordered U-24 into firing position. Able to surface, due to the cover offered by the inky black night and ferocious storm, the *Formidable*'s course, speed, distance and bow position were plotted, using a combination of visual observation and a series of complicated trigonometric telemeter ranging calculations, enabling the U-Boat to help calculate the distance and angle of the target ship's bow. Completely unseen by the British fleet, U-24 was then able to manoeuvre into a perpendicular attack course and commence its torpedo run. The torpedo tubes were flooded in preparation, and the order given to fire number one torpedo.

The risk of detection, and the greater speed of the British ships, usually required the U-Boats to launch their deadly arsenal of C35 torpedoes from a distance of around 1,600 feet. This, of course, increased the potential of miscalculation or of missing the target altogether. However, the cover offered by the storm clouds and the huge swells gave the U-Boat's commander the luxury of manoeuvring to within 1,200 feet of the *Formidable* – comfortably within range – before giving the order to fire, 'Rohr eins – los!'

The first torpedo left number one tube at 2.19am. The watchman on U-24 gave the confirmation signal 'torpedo lauft' (torpedo away) as the projectile snaked its way through the water towards the unsuspecting *Formidable.* Carrying eighty-nine pounds of explosive and travelling at three times the speed of the British ship, the torpedo struck *Formidable* at just after 2.20am, just abaft the fore magazine on the starboard side, fracturing the armour plating. Freezing sea water rushed in through the damaged hull, entering *Formidable*'s number 1 boiler room. An unearthly vibration from the impact stirred the crew, still blissfully unaware in their bunks, followed by the briefest moment of silence until. Then, with a terrifying roar, the torpedo exploded, igniting number 1 boiler and rupturing the already damaged armour plating on the starboard hull. Some of the crew initially assumed it was the sound of gunfire. Their first thought was to man the ship's fore and aft guns. Others, with a sense of impending doom, recognised the sound.

Captain Arthur Loxley ordered the immediate closing of the ship's twelve-inch-thick, watertight bulkhead doors. This helped contain the fire from the explosion and the burning boiler, but not the inrushing water. The damage to the hull was already too great. The ship began to list almost immediately, as thirty feet high waves crashed over the decks.

Noticing the listing, Captain Loxley gave instructions to counter flood the port side in an attempt to correct the list, which risked capsizing the vessel; but it was simply too late for any other option. Too much water had already filled the compartments. The piped order was given to the crew, 'All hands muster on the quarterdeck', to wait for the pinnaces and escape barges to be lowered into the water, in the hope that as many men as possible could be transferred into these smaller boats. Each pinnace was equipped with oars and searchlights, but little else. No motor, no shelter, nor supplies; and little defence against the mighty storm that raged in the ocean below.

However, there was no sign of panic among the grim-faced crew. Distress flares were fired and Captain Loxley ordered the *Formidable* to break line with the other British ships and head directly into Lyme Bay, in the hope of reaching land, or at least shallower waters. The storm force winds continued to lash the stricken vessel, as lookouts searched in vain on the starboard side for the U-Boat that lurked in the darkness, hidden somewhere among the huge swells. Captain Loxley and his second-in-command, Commander Charles F Ballard, remained on bridge, calmly attempting to direct operations, and assuring the crew, 'There's life in the old ship yet,' and to 'be British'. The ship's chaplain, Rev George Brooke Robinson, who had been curate at St Mary's in Burton Bradstock before the war, risked his life to go below decks, in an attempt to fetch cigarettes to calm the crew's nerves and boost their morale. His act of bravery was to cost him his life.

Meanwhile, unknown to the British fleet, U-24 changed direction in the darkness to begin a second torpedo run – this time on the *Formidable*'s port side.

Commander Law, on board the support cruiser *HMS Topaze*, noticed that the stricken *Formidable* had broken formation. He ordered his vessel to rush to *Formidable*'s aid.

The other accompanying cruiser, *Diamond*, also attempted to join in the rescue effort, although the huge swells made every manoeuvre fraught with danger. Guided by distress flares and the flickering lights from *Formidable*, the two cruisers made a valiant effort to pull as close to the listing vessel as possible in the hope of picking up survivors, either from the pinnaces being frantically lowered into the water, or those who were clinging to floating debris in the pounding waves.

By 2.45am the ship had developed an alarming starboard list of twenty degrees. All electrical power had disappeared, shorting all lights, and causing the ship's steering and wireless to fail. A second explosion from the boiler room caused the ship to tilt violently and the sailors on the quarterdeck struggled to maintain their footing as the ship pitched and rolled alarmingly.

HMS Topaze was only able to pick up forty-three men from one of the Formidable's pinnaces, as it churned helplessly in the tumultuous seas, before Captain Loxley signalled the *Topaze* away to seek the assistance of a passing liner. Their mission failed. The liner sailed past without stopping. *HMS Diamond* managed to haul a further thirty-seven shivering crewmen aboard before the threat of continued submarine activity hampered the rescue efforts of both cruisers, which were then ordered to re-join the other battleships as they steamed eastwards away from danger. Captain Loxley selflessly ordered the 'Keep Off!' signal to be flashed from the bridge of the *Formidable*, to warn other ships of the possible danger from U-Boats. Standing orders from the Admiralty instructed unaffected ships to steam ahead to avoid the risk of also being torpedoed.

The Royal Navy, Britain's imperial gem, had been surprised by the comparative ease with which its shipping had been sunk by the German U-Boat fleet. Even at this early stage of the war Britain, still raw from the sinking of the *Titanic* less than three years earlier, had already been shaken by the sinking of *HMS Cressy, Aboukir, Hogue, Good Hope, Monmouth, Bulwark, Hawke, Pathfinder, Ampion, Rohilla,* and *Princess Irene*. All told, a total of more than 5,000 sailors had been killed. Worse was to follow in 1915 with the morale-sapping sinking of *RMS Lusitania* and *HMT Royal Edward*.

In the freezing seas of Lyme Bay on New Year's Day 1915, the preservation of Britian's rapidly dwindling naval fleet was seemingly more important than the preservation of human life.

Meanwhile, U-24 resurfaced just 500 feet from *Formidable*'s port side. Kapitänleutnant Rudolf Schneider ordered torpedo tube number two to fire. At approximately 3.05am a second torpedo struck the stricken vessel, close to her bow. A huge explosion caused Number 2 Boiler Room to burst into flame and the ship lurched alarmingly. Debris from the ship showered down on those men already in the lowered pinnaces. Captain Loxley, realising that the end was nigh, issued the order to evacuate, 'Lads, this is the last, all hands for themselves, and may God bless you and guide you to safety.' He then walked calmly towards the forward section of the bridge, lit a cigarette in the darkness, and waited for the inevitable; his faithful terrier dog Bruce stood at his side.

Second-in-Command, Commander Ballard, was every bit as brave, staying at his post until the end. Together with a signaller, the two men kept on sounding the ship's hooter, and firing flares and distress rockets into the night sky in the vain hope it would offer some hope of rescue to those clinging to the severely listing ship.

Many crewmen were still trapped below stairs, while those on the decks were pounded by strong winds and enormous waves, as they unsuccessfully attempted to lower *Formidable*'s remaining small boats from their davits into the water below. Many of the boats were simply smashed against the ship's hull by thirty-feet waves or overturned in the heaving seas, killing every man on board. Number 2 barge rapidly filled with water and sank, killing the three men who had managed to climb aboard. One desperate sailor pushed the ship's piano overboard and clung to it, shouting out, 'A piano's better than nowt!', and desperately hoping it would float. Another man, a stoker by the name of Smithers, jumped twenty feet from the decks into the first pinnace below, smashing through the wooden thwarts and seriously injuring himself. Meanwhile, those already in the pinnace picked up survivors from the water and dragged them aboard. Many of the men were wearing only pants and vests, as they had been asleep in their bunks when the torpedo first struck the *Formidable*.

Those in the second pinnace, being frantically lowered from the rolling battleship, fared no better. While the boat was being lowered overboard into the churning sea, it swung violently in the huge swells, smashing its searchlights and plunging the men into total darkness. As the sailors grabbed the oars and desperately tried to row away, a mountainous wave smashed their helpless small boat against the anchor of the *Formidable*, stoving in the bows of their fragile wooden pinnace. Freezing water flooded in and several of the crew were forced to strip and stuff the holes with their clothing, in a frantic effort to plug the leaks. Others took off their boots and began a frenzied attempt to bail the incoming water out of the pinnace. In the darkness and the numbing cold, the thought of rescue seemed a distant one as their boat was taking on water at an alarming rate, and the men were half-clothed and shivering. It would not be long before hypothermia set in.

Those in number one pinnace lost sight of those in number two in the heavy swells. At 4.45am, two hours and twenty-five minutes since the first torpedo had struck the *Formidable*, the mighty battleship finally rolled, capsized, and began to sink by the bow into the icy seas. Incredibly, as the ship rolled over at an acute angle, several men attempted to climb up to the ship's port guardrail, then, as the ship turned over completely, somehow clamber onto the vessel's overturned hull. Many perished, including Rev George Brooke Robinson, who was sucked under the battleship by a huge swell. Amazingly, Seaman Tom Walker managed to throw himself into the water and grab a piece of floating debris, despite striking his left foot on the upturned ship's propellor. The mind numbing cold prevented any pain and, with several other men, Walker managed to lash himself to the ship's boom in the hope of staying afloat long enough to be spotted and rescued.

With the bulk of the upturned ship now dragged underwater, the *Formidable*'s stern briefly pointed upwards towards the heavens, in a seemingly defiant gesture, before also disappearing under the waves, as she slipped 200 feet to the bottom of the English Channel.

Captain Loxley was last seen with his faithful Airedale terrier Bruce, smoking a cigarette and still issuing instructions from the bridge. In the great tradition of the Royal Navy, he bravely went down with his ship while trying to save others.

For the moment, still asleep in their beds, the population of Lyme Regis were blissfully unaware of the tragedy unfolding at the western edge of Lyme Bay. No radio signal had yet reached the shore, and even if any townsfolk had chosen to venture out into the howling gale that night, it is unlikely that they would have been able to see the faint light from a distress flare over thirty miles away. With the town in total darkness, due to the newly enforced blackout restrictions, and with temperatures plummeting, the comfort of a warm bed seemed the most attractive option in the early hours of New Year's Day 1915.

Meanwhile, the shivering survivors in the two pinnaces, battered by the stormy seas, desperately clung to life. Close by, and unknown to the few remaining men, U-24 surveyed the carnage it had inflicted, before silently submerging, switching to its electric motors, then gliding directly underneath the keel of the rapidly sinking British battleship, before heading back to the safety of the U-Boat's North Sea base in Heligoland...

IF I SHOULD DIE (THE END)

It was now early morning on New Year's Day 1915. Chinks of faint daylight were at last beginning to show, although the huge swells showed no signs of abating. Pinnace number one and number two floated helplessly, the huge waves obscuring them from the hope of being spotted by any other vessel foolish enough to be out in such atrocious storms.

In number two pinnace the men frantically bailed out the freezing seawater with anything to hand. Their boots, their caps, even a blanket. The forty-two foot long boat was heavily loaded with men, but was holed and sitting low in the rough water. Just before the *Formidable* had sunk, an officer on the deck had shouted down to the pinnace, telling them to row towards the lights to the south. The faint and distant lights were probably those of liners or ships in the channel shipping lanes and it seemed the sailors' best hope of survival. The men grabbed the oars and made a superhuman effort, but it was futile. In the freezing conditions, their strength was sapped attempting to keep the pinnace's bow straight as it fought against the current, the strong wind and the huge swells that threatened to swamp the slowly sinking wooden boat at any moment. As they slowly succumbed to the bitter cold, all appeared lost.

Meanwhile, on the first pinnace to escape from the *Formidable*, things seemed almost as hopeless. One sailor had plugged a hole in the boat's wooden hull by sitting over it, while the others rowed frantically away from the scene. As the morning dawned, one sailor tied his white muffler to the end of an oar, then raised it into the sky like a distress flag, in the faint hope that it might be seen above the crashing waves. It seemed like the beleaguered boat's last hope as the hull slipped ever lower in the water.

Then, between 11am and noon, almost nine hours after the disaster, the nearest thing to a genuine miracle occurred. The trawler *Providence* from Brixham spotted the troubled pinnace. The fifty-ton fishing vessel, under the stewardship of Captain William Pullar, was herself making for base to shelter against the raging storm. However, she had been compelled to heave to by the violence of the gales and heavy swells. One of *Providence*'s crew, a young fisherman by the name of Clarke, somehow momentarily saw the bow of the pinnace among the raging waves ahead. Then she was lost to sight behind the rising crests of water. Bravely, Clarke climbed the trawler's rigging, attempting to keep the pinnace in view, shouting to Captain Pullar. *Providence* made four attempts to draw themselves alongside the rapidly sinking boat, before they were finally able to throw a line aboard. The rope was made fast, and the trawler sailed for home, towing the boat astern. Every moment was precious. The crew of the pinnace had only five oars remaining and could no longer make headway. The water level in the boat was rising, but the sailors had managed to keep her steady by fashioning a wooden anchor from the crossbenches and tying it to a length of rope. By then throwing it overboard, they were able to steady the rolling of their damaged vessel against the ebbs and flows of the huge waves that crashed around her.

At the first opportunity, the *Providence* secured the rope over the capstan and hauled the pinnace under the trawler's lee quarter. The seventy-two men, including five marines and the badly injured Stoker Smithers, were then pulled aboard the fishing vessel. Shivering and exhausted, the men (many of whom were without boots and coats) were given food, coffee and tobacco, as the trawler steamed towards Brixham Quay. The breached pinnace was cut loose and within moments it broke up and sank to the seabed.

Eventually, at around 8pm, seventeen long hours after the men had first entered the pinnace, the *Providence* finally arrived at Brixham. By now the evening papers had reported the tragedy and the townsfolk vied with each other to offer support in the form of hot food, dry clothing, and shelter. The recovering sailors sang *Auld Lang Syne* as they cheered their rescuers and remembered their lost colleagues. For a moment they turned their heads seaward, wondering what had become of their comrades on the second pinnace.

Meanwhile, sixty miles away in Lyme Regis, the early evening newspapers carried an official statement from the Secretary of the Admiralty:

The battleship Formidable was sunk this morning in the Channel, whether by mine or submarine is not yet certain. Seventy-one survivors have been picked up by a British light cruiser, and it is possible that others may have been rescued by other vessels.

In a surprisingly frank admission, especially considering
the strict censorship regulations put in place by the
Government from the outset of the conflict (Lord
Kitchener had even banned journalists from the Western
Front), the newspapers promised to add more detail to later
editions. Although editors were instructed to focus on the
positive angle of all stories (such as accounts of survivors
and of heroism), New Year's Day 1915 was a bleak and
worrying time on the 'home front'. Even domestically, the
news was black. A fatal train crash in London temporarily
diverted readers while they waited for more news of the
Formidable's fate.

In the meantime, the crew aboard pinnace number 2
continued to cling to life. The boat was perilously low in
the water, and in danger of sinking. Some of the crew
rowed, although it became increasingly difficult, as fatigue
and numbness set in. Others continued to bail water
frantically with anything to hand. Despite being soaked
to the skin and poorly clad, the men sang to boost their
morale.

The men's faces were frostbitten by the driving sleet.
Cramp, exhaustion, and hypothermia began to take its
toll. Petty-Officer Herbert Bing bullied, shouted at, and
cajoled those men who seemed to be slipping away. To lose
consciousness now would be to die.

It was now growing dark. Lyme Regis was still eight miles
away and impossible to see from a boat so low in the
water, through the swirling mist and huge swells. The sun
set at 4.15pm and, with it, the pinnace was plunged into
darkness once more. It had now been thirteen hours since

the exhausted sailors had deserted the sinking battleship, without food, water or shelter.

Darkness, however, brought with it an unexpected advantage. At 5pm Petty Officer Bing spotted two blue lights through the gloom. Their spirits temporarily lifted, the men rowed towards them, although they struggled through sheer exhaustion. Two hours later, around 7pm, four white lights appeared, then a red light (most likely, the Cobb's harbour warning light). It appears, rather fortunately for the crew of the pinnace, that the observance of the coastal blackout restrictions was being slackly observed in Lyme Regis that night.

Almost simultaneously, Leading Stoker Joseph Taplin spotted a sudden beam of bright white light, approximately three miles off their bow. It was later thought that this brief guiding light witnessed by Taplin was in fact the cinema projector from the Assembly Rooms at Cobb Gate. It seems that the operator had been attempting to fix the troublesome projector and had briefly – and by lucky accident – shone the light through an uncovered window.

Although the beleaguered pinnace was now drifting shoreward, the men's strength had all but disappeared. They were too far to hail the shore with any hope of being heard. Already, fourteen men had succumbed to the bitter cold and died. In an effort to save the remaining souls onboard, by lightening the load, the bodies were buried at sea. Meanwhile, several more still aboard were close to death. With most of the oars smashed or fallen overboard, no food, and only rain to drink, the men could not survive much longer.

Three more hours passed and the crew, completely sapped of strength, drifted to within touching distance of the town. Although those in Lyme Regis had read of the disaster in the evening newspapers, they still had no idea that a few survivors lurked in the darkness just three-quarters of a mile from the shore. It did not seem likely to the townsfolk that any soul could have survived such a storm, and for so long, or that any boat would have put out in the worst weather since the Great Blizzard of 1891, when at least seven ships had been lost in Lyme Bay.

Even so close to the beach, three more potential hazards still faced the sailors aboard the pinnace.

Firstly, a landing needed to be affected at the right spot. Too far east or west, and the boat might have crashed into the more hazardous rocky shoreline, disintegrating on impact. Secondly, if the severely weakened and exhausted crew had made for the comparative shelter of the Cobb it was likely that their small boat would have been dashed by the severe wind and swells against the unforgiving harbour walls.

Finally, luck seemed at last to be on the side of the barely alive sailors. In the gloom they could make out a shingle beach just a few hundred yards ahead. Frantically the sailors summoned their last remaining ounce of strength from somewhere deep down and coaxed the waterlogged boat forward against the outgoing tide.

At that moment, Miss Gwen Harding was walking with her parents, William and Annie Harding, along the eastern end of Marine Parade. They had intended to return to their home, Chirnside in Hill Rise Road, after having been out for dinner. It was now 10.45pm; more than twenty hours since the first torpedo had struck the *Formidable*. Miss Gwen Harding was the first of the party to spot the boat, sitting low in the water, perhaps four hundred yards from the beach. Annie Harding was next to see it, as the sailors onboard the pinnace began desperately shouting for help. Police Sergeant James Stockley, together with PC Rideout, also heard the shouting. Both men were nearby and within a minute they had joined the Hardings on the sea front. They too spotted the boat, and Sergeant Stockley immediately sent PC Rideout to fetch help. Unfortunately, the Lyme lifeboat was out of commission, having been damaged in bad weather a few weeks earlier, and could not come to their assistance. However, by this time, others, who had overheard the shouting and commotion, had joined them on the beach.

As the boat appeared from the gloom, agonisingly close to the shingle beach, the police officer and the Hardings noticed what seemed to be the unmistakeable crest of a German eagle on the pinnace's bow. During the construction of the *Formidable*, the spread-eagle crest of Admiral Lord Rodney (a Royal Naval hero of the American War of Independence and the Seven Year War) had been fitted to various parts of the battleship, including the pinnaces. In a bizarre twist of fate, the crest bore a striking similarity to the eagle crest on the ensign of the Imperial German Navy. Immediately, those on the beach and watching from Marine Parade, hesitated to help, fearing it was an enemy raiding party. Surely, after more than twenty hours in a battered, rudderless and sail less boat, the sailors would not be thwarted at the last moment.

Thinking quickly, Sergeant Stockley hailed the men, 'Are
you English?' When the response came back, 'Yes!', the
rescue effort could begin in earnest. The sea conditions
were rough, however, and the shingle beach far from
perfect for an attempted landing. Nevertheless, in the faint
moonlight (the blackout restrictions were still in force,
despite the sighting of the survivors), Sergeant Stockley
caught the mooring line thrown towards him from the
boat. He managed to secure the rope and shouted to the
men to come ashore. However, only three of the crew
had the strength to climb from the battered pinnace and
struggle the last few steps through the pounding waves and
onto the beach. Another attempted to do so; but was so
fatigued that he fell into the water and under the swaying
boat, which knocked him unconscious. The quick-thinking
police sergeant jumped into the icy water and managed
to drag the unconscious man to safety. Although suffering
from exposure and badly bruised, the man miraculously
survived. Sergeant Stockley would later be awarded the
King's Police Medal for his bravery.

Meanwhile, word had spread quickly, and many more
townspeople had now joined the rescue effort on the
beach, including Mayor Woodroffe and Lyme's Chief
Lifeboat Officer, RW Abbott. The remaining 51 living
crewmembers on board the pinnace were either helped or
carried onto the safety of the moonlit beach. All were in
a pitiful state, suffering from exposure, fatigue, and total
exhaustion. Nine were unconscious. Tragically, six were
already dead, their bodies lying in the icy water at the
bottom of the boat. The bodies of those unconscious and
already dead were placed on the shingle.

The townsfolk hurriedly brought blankets, food, and hot-water bottles to the nearby Pilot Boat Hotel, which rapidly became the rescue headquarters. The unconscious men's wet clothing was removed as quickly as possible, and they were wrapped in hot blankets. Their condition was critical, their bodies stone cold and almost shut down, their pulse virtually undetectable. Brandy was given to those able to swallow. To those unable to do so, Dr Cooper and Dr Spurr administered hypodermic injections of brandy and strychnine. Sadly, three of the unconscious men slipped away during the night and their bodies were placed, alongside the other dead men, in the entrance to the nearby Assembly Rooms.

Those men well enough to be moved were taken in by the people of Lyme Regis. Alderman Harris, Mr Loud, Mr Johnson, Mrs Radford, Mrs Lloyd, Mrs Strapps, and Canon Jacob all provided shelter. Fourteen were lodged at the Pilot Boat Hotel, with the remainder placed at the New Inn, the Three Cups Hotel, and the Royal Lion in Broad Street. The more seriously ill were transferred to the cottage hospital in Mayor Woodroffe's motorcar. Supplies were sent on the 7.33am train from Exeter to assist with the rescue efforts.

As daylight dawned, and the remains of the battered boat on the beach could be properly seen, utter astonishment was felt locally. How could any of the sailors have possibly survived?

Yet, the extraordinary story was to have one more remarkable twist.

The unconscious body of Able Seaman John Cowan had been given up for dead at the Pilot Boat Hotel, and was laid on the floor, ready to be moved to the Assembly Rooms to be placed alongside the other bodies. However, the landlady Mrs Atkins's dog Lassie - with the strange sixth sense possessed by animals, somehow sensed that Cowan was still alive and began licking his face and hands. Lassie continued tirelessly for half an hour, until the dog's warmth and actions revived the Able Seaman's circulation. John Cowan made a full recovery, and the pair became inseparable. Lassie became an instant celebrity, winning the Royal Humane Society's shield and appearing at Crufts. When Hollywood released the film *Lassie Come Home* in 1943, the people of Lyme Regis firmly believed that their Lassie was the inspiration for the story.

However, what of those who just lost their lives in this unnecessary tragedy? Was justice ever done for those men and the lucky few who survived?

An immediate inquest was held at the Assembly Rooms, followed by an official Admiralty inquiry. At the inquest the jury found that the crewmembers had 'died from exposure at sea following an accident which occurred on board their ship.'

The risk of conducting training exercises in the Channel without destroyer escort was deemed 'excessive', and Vice-Admiral Bayly was relieved of command for 'failing to take adequate precautions against submarine attack.'

Questions were asked in Parliament regarding the rumour that German U-Boats may have received clandestine signals from prisoners housed at an alien internment camp at Portsmouth. The legitimacy of U-Boats targeting a training exercise also created much anger; although this outrage would be dwarfed just a few months later, by the torpedoing of the liner *Lusitania*, which sank in just eighteen minutes with the loss of 1,900 British lives.

The inadequacy of the pinnaces to sustain the lives of sailors in the water, for any period of time, seems a staggering omission in the Navy's duty of care for its men. The boats were not equipped with food rations, lifebelts, blankets, distress flares, navigation, bailing equipment, spare oars, or lights. It is almost certain that, with better provision onboard the pinnaces, many more men would have survived that night. Unfortunately, as the Great War progressed, lessons do not seem to have been have learnt. Many more lives would continue to be lost in almost identical circumstances.

In the class distinction prevalent at the time, the roll call of those men lost in the tragedy was always published listing the officers first, followed by the other ranks.

Lyme Regis honoured the men who reached the beach that night, and commemorated those that did not survive. Three men's bodies were returned to be buried in their hometowns. The remaining six were buried at the cemetery in Lyme Regis, with full military honours. Despite the trauma and exhaustion suffered by the men, they were ordered to return to their respective shore stations immediately after the service, without compensation.

A large crowd in Lyme Regis, including the local Boy Scout band, gave the sailors an emotional and rousing send-off.

A large Celtic cross was erected at the grave site in Lyme Regis Cemetery and the names of the six men added, with the following inscription:

William Feldon, Petty Officer, Aged 36
Horace F Bernthall, Stoker, Aged 21

William C Eley, Stoker, Aged 24
William Fawkes, Stoker, Aged 31
Henry Souter, Stoker, Aged 27
Bernard A de P Smyth, Aged 17

Who Lie Buried Here.
They formed part of the crew of HMS Formidable.
Sunk by torpedo attack from a German submarine
On 1ˢᵗ January, 1915.
When 34 Officers and 511 men were drowned.

Tom Walker, the sailor who had been struck on the foot by the *Formidable*'s propellor while trying to escape the sinking ship, then clung to a floating boom for fourteen hours, was discharged four months later as 'medically unfit for naval service.' He later joined the army, perhaps somewhat aggrieved at his treatment by the Navy.

The body of Captain Loxley was never recovered, although rather poignantly, the body of his faithful dog, Bruce, who had stood by his side while the battleship finally disappeared, was washed ashore three weeks later and was buried within the pet cemetery at Abbotsbury Gardens. A small plaque and gravestone there act as a suitable memorial to man's best friend.

The captain of U-24, Rudolf Schneider, received a different sort of justice for the sinking of *Formidable*. After a career in which he successfully damaged or sank scores of British ships, he suffered an almost identical fate. On 13th October 1917, during similarly stormy weather, he was swept overboard from the conning tower of U-87. Although a crewmember managed to drag him back on board the submarine, he could not be revived and was buried at sea.

All told, from a total crew of approximately 750 men aboard *Formidable* that night, only 199 survived. A total of thirty-four officers and 511 seamen were killed. And one dog.

The wreck of *Formidable* was discovered in the 1980s, although the site remains under the *Protection of Military Remains Act 1986* and access is forbidden. The bodies entombed there will never receive a proper burial. It remains a watery and silent grave for the approximately 545 men who lost their lives. Perhaps there is some dignity, if not justice, in that fact.

The harsh realities of the Great War were fully revealed to the peoples of Devon and Dorset on that stormy January night in 1915. Although many men from the Devonshire Regiment, and the six battalions of the Dorset Regiment, lost their lives on the Western Front, the true horror of the conflict at sea will never be forgotten in Lyme Regis or Brixham.

The poet Rupert Brooke wrote his most famous poem, *The Soldier*, while stationed at Blandford Forum in Dorset with the Royal Naval Volunteer Reserve. A few weeks after the sinking of *Formidable*, Brooke completed the poem and left Dorset for the last time. He too would become yet another Naval casualty of the war while serving with Hood Battalion, RN Division. Yet his most renowned piece of prose, *The Soldier*, mentions only the nobility of a solider dying on land, not that of a sailor sacrificing his life at sea,

If I should die, think only this of me;
That there's some corner of a foreign field
That is forever England.

'Justice' was done, and the President of the Immortals
(in the Aeschylean phrase) had ended his sport with Tess.
And the d'Urberville knights and dames slept
on in their tombs unknowing.

From the final paragraph of *Tess of the d'Urbervilles*,
by Thomas Hardy, originally published in 1891.

ACKNOWLEDGEMENTS
AND REFERENCES

This book would not have been possible without the continued encouragement and help of Kevin & Jayne Ramage and the Lyme Regis Bookshop. Thank you for your enduring support. I would also like to express my gratitude to Ellen McBride, Alexa Reid, Dorset County Archives, Dorset Museum and the Shire Hall in Dorchester, Lyme Regis Museum, the Thomas Hardy Society, Sophia Moseley, Bridport Local Historical Society, Marshwood Vale, Tom De Wit.

The following sources of information have also been invaluable in either helping to piece together the stories contained in this book, or for kindly supplying their permission for the reproduction of images and text:

Dorset Constabulary Archives, National Archives Kew, Freshford.com, Charmouth Church, St Andrew's Church Beaminster, capitalpunishment.org, Hansard Archives (House of Commons), Thames Valley Police Archives, Tolpuddle Martyrs Museum, Exeter Memories, U-Boat Net Research Archives, CNRS-SCN, Burtonbradstock.org, Lyme Regis Museum Archives, Weymouthhistory.org, OPC Dorset, the British Newspaper Archive, DC Thomson, Dorset County Museum, Shire Hall Dorchester, Dorset Council Archives, Exeter Crown Court, Genuki, Judiciary UK, BereRegis.org, Royal Navy, Winchester Magistrates Court, National Asylum Records Kew, The Encyclopaedia of Portland History, Ancestry UK, Parkhurst Prison, The Thomas Hardy Society.

And the following newspapers and journals:

Western Press, Shields Daily Gazette, Western Times, Pulman's Weekly, Chard and Ilminster News, Bedfordshire Mercury, Morning Advertiser, Dorset County Chronicle, Sherborne Mercury, Western Gazette, Weymouth Telegram, Dorset Echo, Bridport News, British History Academy, Hampshire Chronicle, Aldershot Military Gazette, Kent Times, Alnwick Mercury, Evening Mail, The Globe, True Sun, The Age, The London Gazette, Exeter and Plymouth Gazette, Poole and Dorset Herald, West Somerset Free Press, Western Chronicle, Southern Times, Taunton Courier, Shields Daily Gazette, Aylesbury News, Dorset Life.

Bibliography of published resources used:

The Book of Beaminster, Letters of Rev EJ Simmons and Beaumont Featherstone, *Baby Farming, A Victorian Horror Story* by Mary Kay McBrayer, *Amelia Dyer: Angel Maker* by Alison Rattle, *Opium and Infant Mortality* (University of Harvard), Devon Hospital Archives, *Dorset Tales of Mystery and Murder* by Roger Evans, *Dorset Murders* by Nicola Sly, *Dorset Murders* by Roger Guttridge, *St Mary Beaminster* by AAG Walbridge, *The Death and Times of John Daniel* by Marie de G Eedle and Raymond E Paul, *Squire's Fundamentals of Radiology* (Harvard University Press), *Wilhelm Röntgen by* Hans-Erhard Lessing, *The Works of Lord Bryon, Crime, Prison and Punishment (1770-1935), The Police Code 1852, The Victims of Whiggery,* by George Loveless, *Midlands Historical Review, Tea Cultures Ltd, The Tolpuddle Martyrs,* (Trade Union Congress), *Walk Round Weymouth,* by MR Skilling.

Companion books to *Jurassic Coast Justice*, also by Mark Bridgeman

The Dark Side of the Dales
True Stories of Murder, Mystery and Robbery
from Yorkshire's Dark Past
£9.99

Blood Beneath Ben Nevis
True Stories of Murder, Myth and Mystery
from Lochaber.
£9.99

The River Runs Red
True Stories of Murder, Mystery and Deception
from Highland Perthshire's Dark Past.
£9.99

Perthshire's Pound of Flesh
More true Stories of Murder, Mystery and Deception
from Perth and Perthshire's Dark Past
£9.99

Blood Across The Water
Blood, Brutality and Betrayal
True stories form the Highlands of Scotland
£9.99